The Conserver Solution

LAWRENCE SOLOMON

The Conserver Solution

A Project of the Pollution Probe Foundation

1978
DOUBLEDAY CANADA LIMITED
Toronto, Ontario

DOUBLEDAY & COMPANY, INC.
Garden City, New York

To Dawn and to her contemporaries

Copyright © 1978 by Lawrence Solomon
Library of Congress Catalog Card Number 78-19216
ISBN 0-385-14533-0 (hardbound)
      0-385-14534-9 (paperbound)

Printed in Canada using post-consumer waste paper by Webcom Limited

Canadian Cataloguing in Publication Data

Solomon, Lawrence, 1948-
  The conserver solution

"A project of the Pollution Probe Foundation."

Includes index.
ISBN 0-385-14533-0 bd.   ISBN 0-385-14534-9 pa.

1. Environmental policy—Canada. 2. Conservation
of natural resources—Canada. I. Pollution
Probe, University of Toronto. II. Title.

HC120.E5S64   301.31'0971   C78-001425-1

Foreword

WHEN LARRY SOLOMON asked me to write a foreword to this book, I agreed readily because I feel that *The Conserver Solution* has an important task to fulfill. There is a great need for a book that deals with the totality of the Conserver Society, rather than one aspect of it. I am happy that the work is squarely set in a Canadian context and that it addresses the difference between the advertising images of our lives and their daily realities. But what I like most of all is that the author has shown so clearly that the understanding of the issues and the choice of activities is not a matter that only specialists can tackle. He has successfully defined and demystified many of the catchwords and phrases that tend to intimidate the non-specialists. This is important, for it is often the jargon and the intentional obtuseness of the experts, not the complexity of the task, that account for public apathy. *The Conserver Solution* is bound to make a major contribution to the public debate about Canada's future and with it, I trust, to Canada's future itself.

Ursula M. Franklin
Member of the Board,
Pollution Probe Foundation;
Former Chairperson,
Committee on the Implications
of a Conserver Society,
Science Council of Canada

Acknowledgements

An attempt to restructure all of Canadian society, to turn many conventional theories inside out, to remedy our massive social problems while solving our persistent unemployment, inflation, and foreign debt; to attempt to do all this while strengthening democratic principles, while furthering the goals of individuals and industries alike, is no small task. Although I would like to take the credit for the conserver solutions to all these problems, conscience dictates that the many contributions of the Pollution Probe Foundation and others be noted.

Naturally, neither the Foundation, nor any of its members, nor anyone else here mentioned, should be held responsible for any inaccuracies, unpleasantries or discordant philosophies in the text. The reader, then, when reading this book and being pleased, should think of the Foundation and those mentioned below; when finding the text boring, naïve, incorrect or distasteful, should direct his wrath toward the author. Those acknowledged below, I am sure, would prefer it no other way.

To Dr. David Brooks and Dr. Robert Tostevin for their distinct and direct contributions to the book, the former for his consuming concern for where we, as a society, are heading, the latter for his inordinate interest in where we're coming from.

Less distinct but of no lesser importance are the contributions of Chris Conway and Adèle Hurley, so keen at seeing trees, and Brian Marshall, adept at finding forests.

To JoAnn Opperman, for starting the process of having this book become a Pollution Probe project and then wisely leaving the Foundation before the blame could be attributed.

To Marilyn Aarons, for finding humour in the manuscript without always insisting it be deleted.

To Jan Marmorek and Norm Rubin, for their strange devotion to getting things right.

To Dr. Arthur Cordell, Bob Crow, Bob Gibson, Marjory Loveys, and Kathy Ochs for finding the manuscript controversial enough to comment on, and to Dr. Peter Victor for taking the conservation measure of commenting before the manuscript was written.

To Cathy Aarons, Dawn Aarons, Monte Hummel, John Negru, and Linda Pim; some for their general support, some for their hard work.

To Dr. Gordon Edwards and Ralph Torrie, for having spent their half-lives creating a critical mass.

And to Dr. Ursula Franklin, the mother of the conserver society, both its spiritual leader and its fountainhead.

The Pollution Probe Foundation would like to acknowledge the support of The Canada Council.

Contents

The Conserver Solution

Introduction
Progress Without a Price

WITH AN INVESTMENT of only a fraction of a penny—the price of one well-placed match—society is often the beneficiary of tens of millions of dollars added to its Gross National Product (the yardstick by which Canada and every other country in the world measure their progress). That match, placed in the hands of an experienced arsonist, can fuel a feverish amount of economic activity: the costs of firemen and their firefighting equipment, insurance monies paid out in compensation for the damage done, payments to demolition crews to level the charred remains, and then to construction crews to rebuild the buildings, moving expenses to temporarily relocate the tenants elsewhere, and then more moving expenses when they need to be moved back.

Someone who lived around the corner from the site of all this activity—if he'd left the country before the fire and returned after all the damage was repaired—might well find it hard to perceive the prosperity that hit his community in his absence. But out bookkeepers would not be so easily fooled—the prosperity would show up in the GNP as a significant plus to our economy. Should a wave of arson sweep the country, it would do much to raise our official standard of living and make us the envy of countries less fortunate than ourselves.

The Gross National Product does not measure the Gross National Progress. Included in the Gross National Product, along with the things we value, are all those necessities that we'd be just as happy not to have to bear: the costs of pollution and the costs of pollution abatement equipment; rising health costs; welfare payments; police protection; insurance payments; costs associated with joblessness and societal diseases and death.

If these costs (many, particularly the social costs, soaring out of control) were subtracted from the benefits tabulated in the GNP we'd find that much of our progress is pretence, our system of accounting incredibly self-deceptive and self-defeating. As a society, we've forgotten what we're measuring.

Our economy has become very skilled at expanding, at growing in almost any conceivable way. It has been less skilled at distinguishing good growth from bad. Our economy has learned how to be efficient at producing more without bothering to ask if it was efficient to produce more, or if greater efficiencies couldn't be had by wasting less and conserving more.

In energy, and in many other resource areas, we are approaching boundaries in what can be accomplished through more and more production. At the same time we are finding uncomfortable the potential consequences of continuing needlessly in our present breakneck fashion. These concerns provide the thrusts toward the conserver society: recognition that finite resources are being used as if they're infinite, that self-correcting mechanisms in our society aren't working, that social inequities aren't being redressed.

A conserver society wants only to be more efficient by being less wasteful, to be more equitable by having each segment of society assume its share of responsibility. A conserver society wants only to be self-sustainable and wholly regenerative—to assure its own survival by keeping its options open and being mindful of the natural and unnatural constraints we live by.

With one short exception—an aberration of one or two centuries over the entire timespan of human existence—man has followed conserver principles. Scrap copper, iron, and other metals were melted down and recast; old rags were commonly collected for paper-making; wool garments and other materials were respun and rewoven into new apparel and other textile products. Whatever wastes man produced were natural wastes and either used for fertilizer or easily recycled by nature.

We are that exception.

For the first time in human history we have begun to produce unnatural wastes. New chemicals are being created at the rate of 6,000 a year. Many are not found in nature, and when nature is asked to dispose of them she simply doesn't know how.

For the first time in human history the existence of man, nature, earth as we know it, is no longer assured. Readily-available plutonium—the waste from nuclear power plants—or cobalt bombs not yet produced—could guarantee the end of the human race, either by design or by accident.

For the first time in human history the ecological balance has been undermined, and with it the economic balance. We've succeeded in taking more out of our system than we've put in, succeeded in cooking the books to make it look as if prosperity can be had without responsibility, as if our wealth can be separable from our health and the health of our environment.

Treating the globe as an unlimited gold mine, our mines as manna from earth, our natural resources as objects of plunder, we've opened a Pandora's box of economic plagues, social disruptions, ecological calamities. The fault lay not in opening the box but in the way it was opened: mindlessly, with rationalization substituting for reason; arrogantly, without concern for the consequences to befall others.

Our social structure is no longer considered sacred, and our economy expected to suit its needs. For the first time social needs are expected to conform to economic needs and people are seen as the source of problems. They get sick, and need medical care. They become unemployed, and demand unemployment insurance benefits. They become educated, and don't want to work sweeping streets. People, as unemployed, as inefficient, are treated as waste products, as problems our economy must somehow dispose of. The economy no longer exists to make people prosperous; people exist to make the economy work. The result has been a steady fraying of our economic and social fabric.

The irony is that a conserver society allows for economic growth. In fact, it is the only basis for sustained economic growth. Without assured supplies of energy (which we no longer have) and assured supplies of mineral resources (which we no longer have) economic growth cannot be assured. Our progress is illusory—woefully short-term and won at the expense of some other part of our system.

Conserver principles only reconcile our environment with our economy; our ends with our means. Having a base from which we can progress without later being pulled back can let us systematically solve our present economic problems—unemployment, inflation, and our foreign debt—while assuring a sound future economy.

We have the capability today to begin phasing out all non-renewable forms of energy, such as gas and oil, and uranium, and begin phasing in a 100% renewable energy base, one founded on energy sources that will never run out on us. Hydro-electric power, solar energy, and others can meet all of our energy needs without ever threatening to disappear. We can begin phasing out our near-total dependence on continually depleting natural resources and begin phasing in a 100% recyclable economy, where our used resources are diverted from the dump and recycled for society's use. And we can strive for ever-increasing efficiencies, for doing more with less, for starting in earnest to unleash the imponderable potentials in the human mind, to produce an environmentally safe and economically sound place we'll be proud to pass on to our children.

But we have to start now, or our room to maneuver will soon close in on us. For the same reason that many of the dilemmas we face today are caused by decisions made in the past, our dilemmas of the future will be the direct result of many of the decisions we take now.

Entire subdivisions, for example, are being built to be heated electrically. Every electrically-heated home that's built today is going to require electricity for the next 30 to 50 to 70 years. Home heating is one of the most inefficient uses of electricity imaginable, and future supplies of electricity are in doubt, yet we are locking ourselves into a future dependent on this form of energy. We could be locking ourselves into a future energy crisis.

Governments are elected for limited terms, which gives them a limited vision. If the results of a government's program won't show themselves before the next election, the program will have low or no priority. The vision of individuals and industries rarely reaches a farther horizon. Our present planning structures are almost all near-sighted and short-lived. Human cycles, once well integrated into nature, are now out of synch with life cycles. We have developed modern ethics that bear no resemblance to the rules that govern our biosphere and are learning that as we try to impose these ethics crudely and out-of-phase our biosphere is returning the insult.

PART ONE

Separating Fact from Fiction

1 *Early Wastrels*

WHEN MAN WAS a primitive savage, without scientific knowledge of what was good or bad for him, he relied on primitive moral codes to tell him how he should behave. Fiji islanders, for example, believed that the turtle was holy and could not be eaten lightly. Turtles could be caught only with the tribal chief's approval, and then only on certain festive occasions, with special nets, and then only by certain tribal members. Because of all these restrictions the seasonal take of turtles was held to between 50 and 100 per kingdom.

To have taken more, these savages believed, would have been a violation of the moral order of nature that linked the number of turtles in the sea to the number that could be captured. Waste was prevented by adherence to these limits: it was taboo for an islander to catch a turtle for supper, feast on a flipper or two with his family, then let the rest spoil in the tropical heat.

As Fijians became less backward, they gradually cast off their old customs and caught on to doing things in more modern ways. Superstitions surrounding the sanctity of turtles were slowly shelved, until finally, in this century, the turtle became fair game. Anybody can now hunt turtles for sport or commerce, using the most sophisticated fishing techniques available. As a result the once-protected turtle has now all but disappeared, and the Fiji islanders presently face the extinction of their turtles . . . the loss, the waste, of an entire species.

Primitive codes of behaviour not only prescribed what could not be wasted; they also dictated the way waste would take place. Among the world's best wastrels were our own Kwakiutl Indians of Vancouver Island, who practiced potlach (the custom of amassing wealth for the purpose of disposing of it) with a passion. Known then as "keeping up with the Kwakiutls," potlach was a ritual competition for status. Since the Kwakiutls couldn't buy new cars and appliances every year (which would have involved disposing of the old ones) they contented themselves with getting rid of their late-model canoes and crafted ornaments, either by giving them away as gifts (a form of trade-in) or burning them (similar to junking).

The Kwakiutls differed from the latter-day Joneses in one fundamental respect: unlike the Joneses, there was a point at which enough was enough. Waste was important, but not in itself. Potlach had its social function to perform.

More spectacular than sending some canoes up in smoke were human and animal sacrifices—the ultimate waste performed by virtually all primitive communities and ancient civilizations. The sacrifice of living souls was not entirely wasteful, however. For one thing, it took place only on ceremonial occasions and fulfilled a cultural and religious need. For another, the animal sacrificed was often eaten. Zeus, for example, the god of the ancient Greeks, happened to prefer those cuts least valued by the Greeks bearing him gifts, which left the choice cuts for his mortal subjects.

The coming of Christianity kept up the quaint customs limiting waste. During medieval times in Britain, people did not own but merely held God's land as a temporary trust. Customs varied from place to place, but restrictions rooted in religion were always the rule. In one village, nuts could not be gathered before September 1 (nutday); rushes could not be cut before September 26; and the bracken used for thatch and bedding could not be sheared until early October. Wood, the main fuel, was carefully protected. Although the Church owned vast tracts of land and leased much of it for local use, it forbade taking an axe to a tree. A typical lease would allow tenants (usually nobles) only to "lop and crop" for repairs to fences and hedges. Standing timber was taboo. Even on the commons, which was public land reserved for all, only dead wood was allowed to be gathered.

Then man lost religion, and with it his fuel supply. As the power of the Church waned the state confiscated Church property, selling much of the land to devout speculators. These men understood how to make the economy work. One merchant bought state land for 41 pounds and achieved a shrewd return of 109 pounds, simply by stripping 46 acres of timber for sale as wood. Ridding the land of lumber became a national preoccupation.

The energy crisis that resulted from the widespread deforestation of land was solved by the widespread use of coal, a fuel previously frowned upon by Christian nature lovers. Unlike farming, which meant caring for nature, mining had been viewed as a rape of nature. Coal had another black mark against it as well: craftsmen despised it because it dirtied their works. As coal spread from Britain to the rest of Europe, the concern for beauty in material goods and in the human environment weakened. Concern for quality was replaced by concern for quantity. Religion's loss was science's gain.

Much as lawyers are trained in getting around man-made laws, man became trained in getting around nature's laws. Mastering nature became the aim of science. To understand her, nature began being explained in terms of her mass and motion and other physical qualities—in terms of anything that could have a number attached to it.

It was around this time that the term "rate of growth" first appeared. Quite rightfully, it was used to describe the coal industry which, utilizing the inventions of science, provided the fuel for the Industrial Revolution a couple of centuries later.

Before the Industrial Revolution, before we acquired the technological capacity to produce goods at a rate far surpassing our ability to consume them, widespread waste was almost unthinkable. Surplusses, when they showed up, tended to be small and unpredictable, dependent on military plunder or the size of the harvest. Getting rid of surplusses was hardly a central preoccupation, and took on imaginative and idiosyncratic forms, such as potlaches and feasts. With waste part of the general scheme of things, it became useful and so no longer wasteful. The early wastrel may not have valued efficiency, but by appreciating waste, unbeknownst to himself, he was highly efficient.

The modern wastrel does not generally value waste in itself. While professing to value efficiency his waste is of an order of magnitude that is often inconceivable to him and irreconcilable with his view of himself as an efficient, rational, and sensible being. The average Canadian throws away 300 pounds of food per year, more than people in some parts of the world eat. The amount of garbage we produce each year is increasing with no let-up in sight. North Americans now throw away enough refuse each year to construct a wall 200 feet high and 75 feet across along the entire Canada-United States border.

The myth that man can be somehow efficient in the face of all this inefficiency is not unlike our belief that eliminating the inefficiency will somehow be translated into either a reduction of wealth or a curtailment of civil liberties—a curtailment of our democratic, God-given right to waste.

2 The God-given Right to Waste

"THOU SHALT NOT Waste" is not one of the Ten Command-ments. And as long as we continue to recognize property rights, it's not likely to be a prohibition of a conserver society either. Wasting what's our own (as long as it's our own) may not be wise, but it's something only those on a soapbox would try to stop. Whether as individuals we decide to throw our dishwash-ers out with the dishwater, or as a society we choose to build better dams for our beavers, to waste is the prerogative of the waster.

It's important that this remain so. For one person, buying a Chevrolet might seem wasteful when a Honda gets far better mileage. For another, driving a Honda is irresponsible when public transit can do the job. Getting good value (not wasting) can include, for different people, price, durability, style, status, comfort, and a host of other factors. The motive behind a purchasing decision could be almost anything. Judging those motives is too complex for any but the astrologers. Fairer to assume that the motives for people's actions are reasonable, and that they have the right to waste, or not, as they choose. It's only democratic.

The right to waste is not absolute, however. One man's waste may be another man's garbage. It won't do for a cigarette smoker to flick his ashes onto your carpet, no matter how much more convenient it may be than finding an ashtray. Or for a factory smokestack to sweeten your supply of oxygen with sulphur, even when it's done in the name of productivity. Pollution that affects the person, such as the cigarette ash, or pollution that affects the public, such as the sulphur-emitting smokestack, is waste that affects people other than the waster. The costs are no longer being paid by the one who decides to pay them—others are being forced to share in them. This becomes an infringement of their property rights.

To have the right to waste something, a person must own it completely. To own it completely, he must pay for all its costs. Once full ownership exists, an individual can waste what he wants, willy-nilly. He has already seen to it his pleasures won't impinge on his neighbours. All else being equal, he is only exercising his free will.

Some people waste because they don't know any better. They are just not aware that for every minute in winter they keep their front door open while letting out the dog, their house temperature can drop a full degree or more. Or they don't know that leaking taps in one house alone can waste 10,000 gallons of water over a year. If they knew it, they might do something about it. But this kind of information is not readily available. It should be basic information, as commonly known as our body temperature or the length of time it takes to boil a three-minute egg.

Other people waste because they're lazy. They know it makes sense to wrap up leftovers after a meal but find it less taxing to throw the food out instead. They wouldn't mind lowering the thermostat at night to save fuel, as long as they didn't have the responsibility of remembering to do it. These people are often sympathetic to the concept of conserving; they recognize it's in their economic self-interest. Although they haven't the wherewithal to follow through on their own, they would be willing to pay for technology to do it for them. The technology could be as simple as a timer attached to their furnace thermostat, regulating the temperature for them automatically and paying for itself in a matter of weeks.

But the abilities of technology are often harnessed in the opposite directions. Because of the designs of our cities and the designs of our products, people are forced to waste. It would be a practical impossibility for many suburbanites to buy a pound of butter without the use of a 3,000 pound car. It is impossible for almost anyone to go through life without purchasing gross overpackaging along with the product he wants.

Then there are those who waste because they enjoy the luxury of wasting. Filthy rich or nouveau riche, waste is status to them, proof they're not in the position of having to pause before making a purchase, or disposing of it. A lot of waste implies a lot to waste. They waste for the sake of it, but they don't always realize what they're wasting. In a very real sense, what they're wasting is other people's time.

Increasingly, our ability to recycle the materials in goods is improving. Soon, virtually all materials will be efficiently recycled by being returned back to their original state or by being converted into energy—they won't be wasted at all.

What will be wasted is the labour—someone else's time—that went into creating the original goods. When the labour in those goods is destroyed before its usefulness is gone, the value of that labour has been reduced. It has been devalued, denigrated, degraded.

Whether a professional or a blue-collar worker, no one likes to see his work degraded. A lawyer who draws up an elaborate contract only to have it ripped up when his client changes his mind gets a sinking feeling in his stomach, no matter how generously he's been paid for his work. The factory worker who sees the products he helps put together end up in his neighbours' trash cans feels cheapened by it, despite the theory he may have heard that throwing away goods creates employment.

Unless a person is directly affected, he doesn't usually identify with the one whose work is being scorned, he identifies with those able to waste. If wasting were seen for what it is, it would not be accorded the same status it presently enjoys. Status-seekers would have to abandon the myths surrounding the right to waste and express themselves some other way, perhaps by relishing the role they'd have in a conserver society.

3   *Myths of Conservation*

IN 1491, CHRISTOPHER Columbus had a big job ahead of him. He had to do a lot of planning for his trip, talk the Queen of Spain into paying for the expedition, buy just the right kind of provisions and equipment and convince sailors and navigators of the advantages of joining his crew. His job wasn't made any easier by everyone explaining to him why it couldn't be done. First, they'd explain, because the world was flat, if he sailed too far away from shore he'd fall over the edge, where the monsters lived. Second, even if the world was round (here they were humouring him) when he got to the other side, which was the underside, he would fall off. There were other reasons his trip was ill-considered too, all based on equally sound reasoning.

The reasons were considered sound because those who offered them had heard them many times before. Over the years they had acquired a certain amount of respectability, and anyone able to speak the language could cite them with great authority. But though respectable opinions, they were just opinions, myths that got in the way of new discoveries, obstacles in the path of progress.

The idea of the conserver society is faced with modern-day myths, and because it affects so many more aspects of life than a mere ocean voyage it has generated many more of them. Blind belief in these myths, by clouding perceptions of the present, limits understanding of the future.

Conserving energy means freezing in the dark

Only for masochists. Unless you're comfortable in a cool environment, there's no need to be inconvenienced while conserving energy. Most of the energy we use to heat our houses, for
example, escapes to end up heating our outdoors. Cut down on
this waste through insulation and better design of new houses
and we can save energy and money without feeling sinful when
the thermostat stays at 21°C.

*If companies were able to save on materials so that products
could be made cheaper, business would already be doing it*

Twenty-five percent to 30% of the steel used to produce the
ordinary can (which is made of three pieces) could be saved by
using a different process (called the two-piece drawn and
ironed process). In the milk carton business, one manufacturer
produces a one-half pint milk carton that's different only in
that it's a little bit taller and a half inch narrower than the
regular one-half pint container. This minor design change uses
31% less paper and 16% less coating for the paper. Despite the
enormous savings possible in these areas and others, for most
companies it's business as usual.

Canada has virtually unlimited agricultural land

Don't be fooled when looking at a map of Canada. Only 6% of
our land area is fit for cultivation, giving us about the same
amount of agricultural land as California. But this comparison
is deceiving too, since our cold climate and short growing
season yield an average of 1,700 pounds of produce per acre,
compared to 4,000 pounds per acre in California.

Even the 6% isn't sacred. Our amount of agricultural land
has actually been decreasing because our suburbs have been
expanding and the land lost tends to be the very best agricultural land we have. Of our remaining 24 million acres, another
6½ million are expected to be ploughed over in the next 25
years.

Companies will never agree to conserver policies

Premier William Davis of Ontario fell for this myth too, until he got together with 45 of the presidents of his province's leading corporations. Their vote was unanimous: get tough on energy conservation. Most critical was the president of Shell Canada, who called for all the things Davis didn't want to hear: more stringent laws to reduce highway speed limits, higher insulation standards for new buildings, and performance standards for new appliances.

Solar energy may make sense for Florida, but it won't work in the cold Canadian climate

Feeling is believing. It only takes one touch of a solar-heated home's hot-water pipe to convince anyone of the practical power of the sun. Outside it may be 40° below, inside it's warm and snug. Solar systems are very dependable. In the cold, cars may not start when you want them to but there can always be hot water in the tub for your bath (cloudy days included).

Noise pollution doesn't really hurt anyone

Tell that to someone living near an airport. Noise pollution not only hones people's nerves to a fine edge; it hurts in the pocketbook. House prices have depreciated by as much as 45% when airports were located conveniently nearby, and busy city streets are in less demand than quiet cul-de-sacs.

Unlike other forms of pollution, noise pollution does not cause cancer. It only leads to loss of hearing. This hazard has become so common schoolchildren are being advised by health authorities to wear earplugs in noisy surroundings.

There's no point in trying to conserve energy in homes when most energy is wasted elsewhere

Conservation begins at home. An effective program of energy conservation in buildings alone could, over the next 20 years, conserve about as much energy in Canada as any new conventional sources of energy are expected to produce. In just one province (Ontario), for example, installing devices that control hot water systems automatically (called ripple control) would save enough energy to eliminate the need for an entire nuclear plant—at one tenth to one twentieth of the cost of building that plant.

If the management of a company were truly concerned about the pollution it was causing, it would put a stop to it

Company structures are often convoluted, with areas of responsibility poorly defined. A report from a study of management behaviour, in which the executives of a company were interviewed, included this remarkable revelation: "although each interviewee recognized his organization's role as a polluter, none either was acting in a way which would be interpreted (at least in a general sense) as causing the pollution, nor was any individual in a position to end or to significantly change the process.

"In a lengthy discussion with the president of the corporation, it became apparent that the man who occupied the role of president was just as concerned about the pollution as the people who were standing outside of the front gate with vindictive signs. He indicated his love for nature and discussed at some length his particular hobbies, which included forestry, bird watching, and a number of other kinds of activities which appeared to be, at least on the surface level, incongruous with the behaviour of his organization. Further interview sessions with executives, middle managers, and finally rank-and-file workers of the same organization confirmed this finding. Members of the organization consistently were in opposition to the pollution which their company was generating, but at the same time they were content to continue their day-to-day existence as contributors to the very problem which they opposed.

"One respondent commented that it was only a matter of time until the plant in question utterly despoiled its entire surrounding area and that it was a "real crime" since the area was at one time a beautiful national resource.

"When questioned further about his personal response to the

situation, he stated he was powerless to stop the process but that he had purchased a second home (out of the immediately surrounding area) and was planning to move as the effects of the plant became ecologically overwhelming." (David R. Frew. *Academy of Management Journal*)

Idealists who want to eliminate pop cans don't care about the jobs that would go down the drain

Cleaning up the environment usually creates jobs, and the pop can controversy is no exception. In Ontario, for example, about 800 jobs would be lost in the pop can business if consumers sipped their sodas from refillable pop bottles instead. But about 2,000 jobs would be created in the bottle industry, for an overall increase of 1,200 jobs for the provincial economy.

Electricity is the fuel of the future

Living better electrically is already an idea of the past—it is just not efficient to use electricity for fuel when other sources are better suited to the task. Electricity is most efficient in lighting, turning motors, running appliances, and certain specialized industrial applications—only about 10% of our energy needs are usefully met by electricity.

We can run short of gas or oil, but running short of other resources, such as minerals or water, can never happen

It's already happening. A world-wide shortage of all resources is developing. Canada and the United States are starting to feel the pinch in many minerals that were once readily accessible, and the inaccessibility of water is limiting U.S. plans for coal liquefaction and other energy developments in the Rocky Mountain states.

A conserver society would become a bureaucratic nightmare

If it did, it wouldn't be a conserver society. To some, we

already have a bureaucratic nightmare. A conserver society would eliminate many of our present bureaucracies, and replace others with institutions of its own. We need agencies to determine efficiency standards, for example, on which to base our purchasing decisions.

But the bureaucracies don't have to be run by governments, and they don't have to become nightmares. By letting industry and the public play a larger role in determining their own affairs our burgeoning bureaucracies can become a thing of the past.

Nuclear electricity will generate jobs as well as energy

If we're interested in creating jobs, nuclear expansion is one of the worst decisions we can make. Per dollar spent, there are more than twice as many jobs to be had from solar technologies, and four times as many in conservation.

Nuclear energy is the cheapest form of energy

Nuclear energy never looks cheap even by government accounts, but its cost can look reasonable if we don't consider everything involved. For example, the cost of the transmission lines needed to get the electricity from the power plant to the home is often forgotten. When all the costs are counted nuclear energy becomes nobody's bargain, ending up twice as expensive as regular electricity and 20 times as expensive as saving an equal amount of energy through conservation.

Canada is one of the great food-producing nations of the world. Running out of food is the last thing we'll ever have to worry about

It depends on our diet. We export more food than we import, but only in three commodities: wheat, feed, and dairy products. Our self-sufficiency in food ends there. In fruits and vegetables, in meats, in sugar—in all others—we have been importing more than exporting and doing so in increasing amounts.

We can't survive without more foreign investment

We can't survive with much more of it. Despite popular belief, only the poor countries attract massive amounts of foreign investment—it's the rich ones that do the investing. As with other things, the rich get richer and the poor get poorer. Canada's ability to attract foreign investment has given us the largest foreign debt, larger than any other country in the world. We've now reached the stage where we're borrowing money just to pay the interest on our debt.

Advertising is important for competition in our free market system

It may have started out that way, but advertising now prevents competition and helps preserve the *status quo*. Most brands of toothpastes, for example, new or old, are owned by a very few companies. Advertising, because it's so persuasive, also prevents competition based on price. Companies now set their own prices and gear ad campaigns to sell at those prices. Instead of the free market determining price, advertising does it in North America as effectively as the state controls prices in Eastern Europe.

The limits to growth are determined by the amount of physical resources we have

Only partially. Offsetting our limited resources is a perhaps unlimited reservoir of intellectual capital. While we may stop finding more resources, we need never stop using them more efficiently. The old trans-Atlantic cables, which took up 175,000 tons of copper, have been replaced by one-quarter ton commerical satellites that can out-perform them in every respect. The 175,000 tons of copper was then made available for reuse. Similarly, the strength of aluminum—18,000 pounds per square inch—can be almost doubled to 32,000 pounds per square inch merely by adding a small amount of copper.

If recycling were more economical than using raw resources,
businessmen would be the first to take advantage of the savings

Which businessmen? In the pulp and paper business, for example, the main recyclers are the same companies that chop the
trees down, convert the lumber to pulp and then manufacture
the paper. But they recycle only when they're short of the raw
materials. If they started recycling all the waste paper they
could get, the division of the company that fells the timber
would suffer, causing lower overall profits to the company. The
situation is further complicated by tax laws that favour the use
of raw resources, and freight rates that subsidize raw resources
while penalizing the shipment of scrap materials.

More durable goods will mean less employment

With that logic we should be making goods to break down the
day after they're purchased. More durable goods would not
mean fewer jobs but it could mean different jobs. Autoworkers
who make long-lasting cars, for example, might shift to producing buses. As long as there are products people want, there
will be work for people to do. But the production of more
durable goods could also mean more sales to people who value
quality, both in Canada and abroad. Here, longer-lasting goods
will mean more employment.

Since one principle of a conserver society is doing more with less,
or increasing efficiency, companies have always been following
conserver principles

Some companies have, but too often the efficiency gained by a
company has been won by imposing inefficiencies on other
parts of our system. Coal mining looked very efficient to companies when the costs of Black Lung Disease were allowed to
be paid for by miners.

Efficiency, in a conserver society, means total efficiency.
Doing more with less when others are carrying the load is an
altogether different principle.

Canadians are as efficient in using energy as anyone else

Where energy is concerned, Canadians are efficient only at misusing it. We waste more energy, per person, than any other country in the world. The affluent European countries, for example, use half the energy we use and have a higher standard of living. Compared to Sweden, a country whose climate is very similar to ours, we use 50% more energy with nothing positive to show for it.

Solar energy may be fine for homes and greenhouses, but it will never be able to replace the need for electricity

Solar energy is easily converted to electricity, but the costs are still too high to be commercially feasible. At this writing, solar-generated electricity costs three dollars per watt, or about six times the cost of competing sources. But the costs have been dropping by half each year for several years, and will be competitive within three years if this rate continues. Far likelier, however, is a major breakthrough in this technology which will make solar-source electricity competitive for many applications in an even shorter period of time. The rate of innovation is accelerating so quickly that costs have dropped twice in the course of writing this book, and could well have dropped again by the time you read this.

Recycled paper is inferior to new paper

There is no difference whatsoever between the two, either in looks or in strength. The paper in this book, for example, is made of recycled stock. In fact, 20% of the paper we use is recycled, usually without our knowing it.

Unrestricted growth is good

Cancer, crabgrass, and rats all breed at alarming rates—often they expand until the system that supports them dies. Too much of even a good thing, such as candy, can turn the stomach. In our economic system because of incentives some companies and industries tend to grow until they're so large they can throw their weight around at the expense of other companies and industries. At the same time, they often become so inefficient and cumbersome that they demand more support from governments to keep them propped up. We're left with the unhappy choice of letting a company or industry we've come to depend on go under, or continuing to favour it at the expense of other potentially viable enterprises.

Canada's domestic market is too small for us to develop a manufacturing base

Don't tell that to Denmark, Belgium, Switzerland, and other countries with smaller populations than ours. They might then develop an air of resignation and find their manufacturing industries start faltering too. Britain, Germany, Italy, and France each manufacture many lines of cars. Although our population is about half of each of theirs, we don't even produce one. Sweden, with a population that's two thirds our own, manufactures two makes of cars.

Conservation means making do with less

Put another way, conservation means doing more with less. This often takes some thought. The match boxes the E. B. Eddy Company used to produce, for example, had two strips of sandpaper, one on each side. It took a top executive to see that if one strip was used instead of two, the company could save money. Despite the risk that customers would not tolerate the inconvenience of sometimes having to turn the box over, the money to be made was so great the decision was taken. The company did not go bankrupt.

Conservation can also mean doing less with less. This takes less thought, but it will work just as well for whoever wants less, or wants to think less.

There isn't enough energy from the sun to let us do everything we need to do

One way or other, the sun is virtually our only energy source. It makes water move (which gives us hydro-electricity) and the wind blow (which can give us wind-generated electricity). More direct sunlight falls on our homes than we need to heat them, and the amount of solar energy collected and stored by wild vegetation alone is more than 80 times the total energy requirement of all mankind. Even in the industrialized countries direct solar energy contributes far more to national economies (in uses such as agriculture and forestry) than any other single energy source.

Canada is too small a country to develop its own technologies

Most significant inventions come not from mammoth organizations but from private entrepreneurs, and do not require huge amounts of money. Even industrial technologies usually are created by individuals. This means that the little guy, or the little company, or the little country, is at no disadvantage in pursuing independent research. Historically, this has been the case for Canada, but it's also been the case that we have failed to capitalize on our inventions. Some examples:

- Alexander Graham Bell's telephone was not eagerly received in Canada. George Brown, who owned the *Globe*, bought the rights to the telephone for $25 per month for six months, but then decided it didn't have enough potential to justify a major commitment. Another Canadian company was then offered this invention but also turned it down. Finally an American company, the National Bell Telephone Company took over the United States and Canadian rights and later formed the Bell Telephone Company of Canada.
- George Desbarats did not patent his half-tone reproduction invention although he used it in his Canadian National News for 10 years before it was patented in the United States. Ironically, Desbarats was also the founder of the Canadian Patent Office Record.

- The Kodak developing tank was invented in 1899 by Arthur McCurdy, patented in the United States and Canada and sold to Eastman Kodak in Rochester, who reaped the rewards.
- In 1921 William Stephenson developed a system to send pictures by wire, but Canadian newspapers and electrical companies weren't interested. He finally obtained a British patent and made a commercial success of his invention in Great Britain.
- J. T. Wright developed the electric trolley pole and overhead wires for mass transit. They spread to all the major cities of the world, but Canadian industry failed to benefit.

Other examples of Canadian innovation include the electron microscope and the hydrofoil principle. Of inventions that were developed in Canada to benefit Canadians, the snowmobile and other types of all-terrain vehicles represent one of the few Canadian success stories.

There is no energy crisis

Oil is running out on us, but it won't affect us seriously for another decade or two. We therefore have the option to go full speed ahead until then and crash land, or else start conserving our remaining supplies, and come in for a soft landing.

PART TWO

The Conserver Approach

4   *The Restraints on Resources*

UNTIL 1975, CANADA was a net exporter of oil. Now we import 300,000 barrels a day, at a cost of $1.5 billion a year. By 1985, we'll be importing 1,000,000 barrels a day to keep our economy lubricated. This will be costing us $5 billion a year. Our known reserves were high a decade ago—8.4 billion barrels—with more assumed to be readily available when needed. We were wrong.

At the beginning of the 1970s, we seemed so successful as an oil-exporting nation that Jean-Luc Pepin, then Federal Trade Minister, couldn't conceive of an energy shortage: "It would be crazy to sit on it," he expounded. "In maybe 25 to 50 years we'll be heating ourselves from the rays of the sun, and then we'd kick ourselves in the pants for not capitalizing on what we had when gas and oil were current commodities." The idea of curtailing shipments to the States and saving the fuel for ourselves—the notion he found "crazy" then—would be given a different reception today. Pepin might even feel *his* policy of shipping away our future supplies to have been crazy, considering the fact that we were paid one-quarter of what those oil resources would be worth a few short years later.

But Mr. Pepin had not cornered the market on short-sightedness, just as his successors are not alone in thinking that what happened to energy can't happen to our other resources. It has always been easier to take our minerals for granted than to worry about the day they will run out—particularly since they have served us so well in the past.

In 1867, the year of Confederation, the mineral industry accounted for 1.5% of our GNP. Its share of GNP rose to 4% by 1945, and to 7% by 1973. Minerals and metals accounted for 20% of our exports in 1950; 30% by 1970. Since the war, the mineral industry has been our most important industry—primary or otherwise. The value of its output has surpassed that of manufacturing, forestry, and agriculture combined.

For a country that depends so much on one industry, we've been extraordinarily complacent about it. We're happy, for example, to sell as much of our mineral wealth as we can, without much concern about finding more later or getting a proper price now. At the same time, a fear lurks that if the minerals aren't sold soon they'll become replaceable by other metals, or tough plastics, or recycled minerals. This view was expressed in a recent report to the Science Council of Canada: "our unmined reserves may become useless if other products take their place, or if major industrial countries develop an [alternate] economy based essentially on [the] metals most abundant in the earth's crust." As a result of this kind of thinking we have been satisfied with whatever we could get.

The irony is that these attitudes, rather than promote Canada's mineral industry, sell it short. They fail to acknowledge the industry's long-term importance both to our economy and to our society. Defying all logic, policies continue to be proposed that may have been sound a century ago but threaten to lead to economic collapse today.

The notion that our unmined minerals may someday soon lose their value would come as a surprise to other countries that depend on them. Rogers Morton, U.S. Secretary of the Interior, in 1974 feared the coming mineral crisis would be worse than the oil crisis. The United States, our main export market, uses 40% of the total world mineral output. The Americans don't have sufficient reserves to satisfy their demands over the next two decades for 47 of the 87 principal commodities necessary for sustained economic growth. They include the essentials: copper, lead, zinc, tin, aluminum, iron, and nickel.

In 1950, the United States depended on imports for more than half of its supplies of four key minerals—aluminum, manganese, nickel, and tin. By 1970, the list had grown to six, with zinc and chromium being added. In 1985, the list will total nine, with iron, lead and tungsten tacked on. At present rates, in 20 years the United States will be dependent on imports for more than 50% of all its metal needs.

The demand for raw materials won't come from the United States alone. Japan, West Germany, and the USSR show a strong and continuing demand for primary resources, and the emerging affluence of many European, African, Asian, and Middle Eastern countries will intensify this demand. The world is expected to require four times as much minerals 20 years from now as it required one decade ago.

A sharp increase in the prices of many minerals and other industrial commodities is inevitable, despite decades of relative price stability. Iron, the most abundant of all metals, with reserves considered effectively infinite (iron makes up 3% to 5% of the earth's crust and 35% of its interior) is expected to quadruple in price. Essential resources that are less abundant could well increase more.

As the industrialized nations become more vulnerable to supply shortfalls, the tenor of trading will become less tempered. International cartels have already formed to capitalize on the coming quandary of the capitalist countries. The CIPEC nations (Conseil Intergouvernemental des Pays Exportateurs de Cuivre), Peru, Zaire, Zambia, and Chile, and others, will be abundantly equipped to control the sources of supply and prices for copper, aluminum, tin, iron ore, and other minerals resources. Third World Countries already control most of the world's known copper reserves. They're unlikely to treat their former colonial masters with any more compassion than their former colonial masters treated them.

Canada did not have to join OPEC to benefit from the oil cartel, and will not have to join the mineral cartel to boost our mineral prices without blushing. But if we do now with our minerals what we did with our oil (in 1972, the year before the oil cartel asserted itself, Canada shipped fully 5% of its known oil reserves to the United States alone) we won't have much left to sell when the price rise comes.

We are sitting on gold mines, and iron mines, and copper mines that have value far beyond the current conventional conception. Like the grandsons who received General Motors and IBM stock before their value multiplied, we can become wealthy merely by knowing enough not to sell the reserves we still have too soon.

Our copper reserves are currently pegged at 16.8 million tons (down 2 million tons from the previous year). If no new reserves are found, projections indicate we will run out of copper that's worth mining within 20 years. Lead reserves are at 9.2 million tons (down 1 million tons from the previous year). If no new reserves are found, projections indicate we will run out of lead that's worth mining within 20 years. Zinc reserves now total 28.1 million tons (down 3 million tons from the previous year). If no new reserves are found, projections indicate we will run out of zinc that's worth mining within 25 years. Nickel reserves are about 7.3 million tons (down from 8 million tons the previous year). If no new reserves are found, projections indicate we will run out of nickel that's worth mining within 25 years.

And on it goes. In most categories Canada's reserves are dwindling yet production keeps increasing wherever it can. It's probable that we'll make new finds, but it's also probable that the new discoveries will come more and more infrequently and become increasingly expensive to mine and process. More significantly, our mineral reserves will increase because, as the price of minerals goes up, mines which aren't considered profitable to work today will become paying propositions. And because technology will undoubtedly discover ways to recover minerals from the ground that aren't now practical to recover.

On the other hand, it's also probable that in the case of one or more of our minerals we've overestimated the reserves, and that we'll find ourselves importing, as with oil, a commodity we were previously thought rich in. Another one of our important earners of income—one of the few our economy depends on—will have been sold out from under us. When that happens, chances are we will pay much more for it than others had paid us. A better business sense would avoid all this.

It is possible that we'll always be able to keep one step ahead of the world's increasingly insistent demand for resources, as we have been doing. Mining methods in Minnesota allowed steel made from 30% iron ore to be competitive with foreign steel from ores having double the iron content. Arizona has been increasing its copper production over several decades through advanced technology and treatment methods. Canada, too, has made significant advances. Iron mines in Labrador and copper mines in British Columbia, each producing low-grade ores, would not be open without technological advances and huge capital inputs.

But it's becoming ever more unlikely—perhaps statistically impossible—that an increased pace of exploration can do much more than buy us a little extra time. We're already going considerably out of our way to find enough raw resources to keep industries going. We're drilling holes in the Arctic and under the ocean floor. Nor is Canada alone in this desperate drive to maintain mineral supplies at a satisfactory level. International organizations are squabbling over who controls the mineral resources of the oceans and of Antarctica. The squabbling intensifies as more governments realize the enormous reserves in these remote areas and the enormous needs they may not be able to meet without them.

Potential shortages loom so large that serious thought is being given to the possibility of mining the moon. Mineral samples already brought back from the lunar surface indicate a wealth of mineral deposits there—deposits expected to be in short supply here.

Elaborate plans exist for delivering vast quantities of moon metals to earth. Plans also exist for moving mineral-rich asteroids into an earth orbit. Miners, living in colonies in space, would use large solar mirrors to melt and refine metal from the mining asteroid. The metal would be formed into ingots, then be shaped into large rafts and sent by space tug to a refinery, also in orbit around the earth. There the ingots would be remelted to form the "foam-metal" components of the atmospheric entry body, and sent to earth.

It sounds promising, but no delivery dates have been set for the first shipments. Transportation costs still have to be reduced by several orders of magnitude. Our hopes are banked on a host of improbabilities coming through. It's much like thinking that if we buy thousands of lottery tickets some have to pay off. Some may, but even then, the only recourse will be to purchase more tickets to get us through the next crisis. This is hardly an impressive way to run an economy. There is no basis here for continued growth. In any event, it's completely unnecessary for economic prosperity.

Mines are not the only sources of minerals at our disposal. The sum total of thousands of years of previous mining now lies above ground, much of it unused and with increasing amounts—today's scrap heaps—being continually added to the inventory. These scrap heaps are not only absolutely dependable sources but we know where they're located (in fact, we can locate them where we choose), we know how to recover the resources in them, and we know that if our economy decides to form a closed loop, with all used resources recycled back into use, there would be little reason ever to worry about our sources of supply again.

5 *Enter the Recycler*

IN A SENSE, no resources are ever lost; nature accounts for all her possessions, whether organic or inorganic. All organic resources contain energy and are converted into energy, either deliberately by us (say by burning timber) or as a matter of course by nature (as dead leaves become fertilizer). But although these organic resources are never lost to nature, they may be lost to us if we use them inefficiently. Nature doesn't much care what those dead leaves fertilize, but we may. Nature doesn't much care where household garbage rots either, but for many communities it is a major preoccupation that has accelerated out of control.

Inorganic resources are never lost for another reason—they have no energy in them to lose (with the exception of radioactive materials) so they remain dumb matter, unsusceptible to transformation, despite the determined attempts of centuries of alchemists. Inorganic materials include minerals (although all minerals are not inorganic) and minerals have one quality in common: they are non-renewable resources. Unlike lumber or food or fisheries or water, once minerals are taken out of the ground they don't replenish themselves.

But neither can they be destroyed. And since they are indestructible they can be reused, or recycled.

Recycling is nothing new. Human beings back in the Iron Age discovered that a metal spear tip bent out of shape from missing its target could be pounded back into shape. If it hit its target it could be scraped clean and reused. Iron Age Man did not waste his scarce resources. Twentieth-century man has been making similar discoveries, and because he's much smarter, he's been making a lot more of them.

Forty percent of North America's (and the world's) supply of copper is recycled from scrap. Forty-five percent of North America's lead is recycled, even though several hundred thousand tons of it gets dissipated in uses such as gas additives. Half of the continent's iron production is based on recycled material, 20% of its aluminum, 25% of its rubber, 40% of its zinc, and 50% of its antimony.

There has been only one reason for all this recycling that's taking place—it's cheaper. The used materials are readily available and already processed from the raw stage. There's no need for grown men to go digging holes in the ground looking for minerals when they're already sitting on top, ready to be plucked.

The hero in the recycling saga is the junk car. Because it provides great quantities of different materials, it has encouraged people to develop ways of getting them back. About 7.5 million cars are scrapped in North America each year and 80% of these are recycled for their metal and material content. In the past three years, more cars have been recycled than have been junked. We've started to mine our old automobile graveyards. The junk car has emerged as the most recyclable and recycled post-consumer product in the history of mankind. Its story deserves to be told.

When a car goes to the auto-shredder, its tires, fuel tank, battery, and radiator are first removed. Then it is literally shredded into fist-sized fragments. At this point it loses its will to resist. A giant suction tube from above lifts out all the low-density materials (the foam stuffing from the seats, rubber, plastic and others) during the actual shredding process. These used to go straight to the garbage sites but with convenient landfill sites used up, the increasing costs of disposal and the increasing volume of materials, they are no longer being considered waste. The Ford Motor Company, for example, has developed a method to convert the foam to new polyurethane foam or to other industrial chemicals right at the auto-shredding location.

After the car has been well shredded, a magnet removes 95% of all the ferrous metals. Because the price of scrap steel has soared as high as $140 a ton, intensive research is working on means of recovering the remaining 5%. Before 1970, what was left—mostly zinc, aluminum, copper, and copper wire, stainless steel and iron—went to the garbage dump. Today, by putting these metals in dense liquids, 95% of this scrap is recovered for reuse. Different metals float in different liquids. They are simply collected in turn and shipped for refining.

Some shredding companies have become so successful at separating out these metals that they've become the shredder's shredder. Most shredding companies in the United States and Canada now ship to a few central non-ferrous recovery sites. One of these has become the world's largest producer of recycled zinc and aluminum, recovering approximately 25,000 tons of each of these metals each year. The modern North American car contains about 85 pounds of aluminum. By the 1980s, to produce lighter vehicles that will meet compulsory mileage standards, cars will contain about 200 pounds of aluminum. By the 1990s, when they're junked and mined, over one million tons of aluminum will be available for recovery each year.

In 1971, only 4% of North American consumption of aluminum was recycled from the automobile. Then came rises in the price of scrap aluminum and rises in the price of energy (aluminum produced from bauxite requires tremendous amounts of energy). Better technologies were developed to recover aluminum from scrapped cars. With the coming availability of aluminum, we'll see the emergence of new and better technologies for its separation and recovery.

Cars now use 150 pounds of plastic. Also for the reason of fuel economy, cars will contain 200 pounds of plastic by 1980. But plastic use is already high. The typical car in the early 1970s was 3% to 4% plastic. When these cars are junked in the early 1980s, there will be over one billion pounds of plastic ready for recovery each year. Methods are being developed to recover plastic for reuse as plastic, to use it as fuel, and to turn it into animal feedstocks. Plastic may even be turned into crude oil. It will be considered too valuable to be thrown away as garbage. For the automobile industry and many others, recycling has become irresistible and the trend toward more and more of it—toward a 100% recyclable economy—has become perhaps irreversible. A course in business administration is not necessary to understand why.

Recycled materials are closer in composition to the final product than are primary raw materials. This gives them a financial edge, because recycling eliminates the primary production phase of our resources. Gone are the costly mining, milling, and processing of ores. Gone, too, is much of the waste and pollution associated with production. In the mining of iron, for example, every ton of ore produced leaves as much as a ton and a half of waste. Recycling bypasses this phase and so bypasses the problem of what to do with that ton and a half. The use of ferrous scrap in steel production also bypasses the costly iron blast furnace (as well as the pollution associated with this process and with the production of coke).

Production that arises from recycling requires less chemical or metallurgical processing than primary production. It can be carried out in plants which are simpler and so require less capital investment. This production is also more flexible because recycling plants can be constructed in much less time than new mining and smelting facilities, and they can be located where they're most convenient. (Ore bodies do not always choose practical sites in which to be found.) The operating costs of recycling plants are lower than primary production facilities, as much as 65% to 75% lower in favourable cases.

A large part of these savings come in the form of badly needed energy. By recycling steel we save about 74% of the manufacturing energy needed to produce new steel from primary ore. For aluminum, the saving is as high as 95%. In terms of a finished product—say an automobile—the final savings are substantial. The bulk of the energy involved in manufacturing a car is the energy required to produce the basic materials. (Manufacturing and assembly combined take up only a quarter of the total.) A car made of recycled materials could save as much as 30% of the total energy bill.

In asserting itself as an economic force, recycling has overcome many artificial economic barriers and disincentives. Freight rates and taxation policy discriminate in favour of the primary producer. The primary producer has the benefit of generous depletion allowances—allowances not available to a producer of the same material but from recycled stock. When these artificial policies (dating back to the last century) are rejected and recycling is put on the same economic footing as mining it will be a solid sign that government recognizes the changes that are taking place.

Recycling can do more than save money while conserving resources. It can also save our surroundings. You don't have to be an environmentalist to object to ruined parklands or the alarming rise in cancer due to poisons in our air and in our water. Yet without recycling our wastes we are destined for more of the same.

We're in the midst of a garbage explosion. A baby born today will generate one million gallons of sewage and 180 tons of trash over his lifetime. Every year, each person throws out 1,500 pounds of garbage—that's three tons for a family of four. At present rates, Canada's garbage will double every 15 to 20 years.

Soon there will be no place to put it. The convenient landfill sites are already scarce. Garbage is now being shipped extraordinary distances only to be dumped. When the sewage is left uncovered it smells, attracts scavengers, and breeds disease-carrying organisms. The open burnings common to these dumps control rat populations (with the exception of Alberta, there are more rats than humans in the provinces of Canada) but threaten life and property.

The amount of poison released at open dumps can be staggering. A single 50-acre site, for example, receiving one inch of rain can yield 1.36 million gallons of leachate, a contaminant that enters water supplies and can harm nearby land. When the garbage is covered by layers of earth at landfills it makes the disposal site more pleasing to the eye and nose, and reduces risk of disease. But the risk remains high, as witnessed by the many lawsuits demanding compensation for damage done to private property and city water supplies.

Landfills produce methane gas as well as leachate. When the gas wafts over to areas of human habitation, it can explode, as one gentleman lighting a cigarette in his apartment was surprised to discover. When the gas stays away from areas of human habitation, it merely represents a danger to vegetation.

Better garbage disposal systems exist, although they are somewhat more costly. Called "sanitary" landfill sites, they involve an engineered method of disposing of solid wastes to minimize environmental hazards. The waste is spread in thin layers, compacted and covered with a protective material. Safer still are "secure" landfills. Here, the wastes are put into containers that separate them from the environment, and then buried underground. This system is used for extremely dangerous wastes: access to the site is restricted and the site is continually monitored.

All the garbage disposal systems devised—including their collection and transportation costs, the manpower costs, the land removed from other uses, the risks to our environment and the risk to ourselves—are designed to return us nothing. The most we can hope for, after paying for these massive systems, is that there will be nothing else to pay because of them in future. It's a no-win plan.

Yet all the ingredients in garbage have value. One person's table scraps could be another person's fertilizer. The metal from a broken toaster can become the metal in a brand new iron.

The largest single material in household garbage is paper—it amounts to 40% to 50% of what we put out for the garbageman. Paper has become so valuable that "newsprint pirates" have been known to sweep city streets the night before weekly paper pick-ups to steal it away from city garbagemen. Municipal budgets have been feeling the pinch.

Paper that is not suitable for recycling can be burnt as fuel, along with most everything else in the garbage can. Incinerating garbage can reduce it to 10% of its volume. The 90%

consumed can make valuable contributions to the energy needs of communities.

Conventional incinerators are on the way out. They're too costly and dirty. (The disposal of garbage is of dubious benefit when it produces pollution in the process.) Replacing them are small, modular incinerators, processing less than 50 tons of garbage per day (the conventional ones process 200 to 400 tons per day). Modular incinerators are better at recovering energy from wastes while having operating costs the same as the larger models, and they can be installed in much less time. They're especially well-suited to small towns. Used in cities, they can be placed throughout communities in groups of four to eight, saving transportation costs.

But garbage will become too valuable even for conversion to fuel. Although there's energy in plastic, the plastic could be worth more in a child's toy. And why burn what can be sold as fertilizer?

In recent times, the value of garbage has been best recognized in crisis situations. During World War II, when mineral production from the ground wasn't enough to meet the metals shortage, we relied on our backup supplies—our junk. When the raw materials crunch came in 1973-74 (due to the oil crisis) we experienced severe shortages in all energy-related commodities and general raw materials. Virtually every metal was in short supply. So were paper packaging products. This period broke down barriers to recycling technologies. Then came the recession, and the situation reversed. The demand for scrap fell drastically, and with it scrap prices. It stopped being economical to collect scrap and so it stopped being economical to recycle.

With each fluctuation in the stock market, the price of scrap fluctuates. Copper scrap can cost $1 per pound one month, 40 cents per pound a few months later. Aluminum scrap can lose more than half its value in weeks while primary aluminum prices stay level.

The collection systems for scrap become lucrative one month, unsupportable the next. It's a business that, at present, has no secure economic base. This makes it more expensive and less efficient than necessary, despite the collection system's ability to deliver goods at prices that make the recycling end viable. If it's profitable for the recycler to produce copper when he pays $1 a pound for it, it should be much more profitable when the copper costs 40 cents.

Although scrap supplies 44% of our copper, 20% of our iron and steel, 50% of our lead and 20% of our paper, scrap is still considered the back-up source. The primary source remains holes that have to be dug hundreds of feet into the ground.

The situation could be reversed.

An economy dependent on recycled goods would have its collection system constantly in place. Besides reducing costs, it would guarantee supplies for the recycler, who would have the security necessary to invest in plant improvements and technological innovations. Recycling our materials would reduce our garbage and streamline our economy—less waste all around.

Instead of storing our backup supplies on the earth's surface, we can store them under the ground. And it isn't necessary to figure out how—that's where they're being stored now. As we need them, to expand our economy, or to export, or to make up material lost in use and production, we can dig them out. Unlike the all-or-nothing collection system we need for recycling, the mining industry is potentially highly flexible. Mines can operate at reduced rates of activity without having to be shut down entirely. Because of this flexibility, they are ideally suited as a support system, one that could co-exist with recycled minerals, while adding to the overall efficiency of the economy.

A national no-garbage policy needs only a distribution system that brings garbage to recyclers. (The distribution system already exists, only it persists in bringing garbage to the dumps.) In some cases, the recyclers will be brought to the garbage. That's the case with the Ford Motor Company's plan, locating its foam recycling plant at the auto-shredding location, and it's the case with recycling of old asphalt. Highways are now being resurfaced on the spot, mostly with materials already in place.

The efficient use of our resources is only good business; only good management. Recycling has made those inroads against impressive odds for no other reason. Continued mismanagement will be harder and harder to justify in a world that's becoming progressively more aware that we are pushing against natural limits.

If we don't conserve our resources, if we continue to waste them, sooner or later we will run out of them. For a country like Canada, this could be especially crucial. We depend very heavily on the export of natural resources for our livelihood. Without a conserver society, we could find ourselves with a resource-based economy and no resources.

6 Conservation and Unlimited Economic Growth

I

MISMANAGEMENT OF OUR natural resources stunts economic growth. This is well understood after the fact. Ignoring the rules of soil management has yielded frustrating results for farmers who didn't believe the rigamarole about rotating crops. Forest resources have disappeared when forest conservation measures weren't taken. The whaling industry lost large money-earners when it depleted the world stock of blue, right, and hump-back whales.

There are a lot of fish in the sea, but not enough for us to take them for granted. In the 1960s, world fishing catches were predicted to increase from the then 60 million tons to one billion tons per year by the year 2000. With the failure of the Peruvian anchovetta catch in 1971 the predictions were laid aside. World catches have been falling ever since as a result of previous overfishing and the growing pollution of coastal waters.

Water itself is easy to take for granted—there are 326,000 cubic miles of it. Ninety percent of it is in the oceans or locked in ice. Only 0.7% is fresh at any given time, and of this, only one sixth is gathered in streams, rivers, and lakes. Within twenty years, the world's population will require 25% of all the earth's surface waters. But when water demand exceeds 10% of surface waters in a given area, its costs rise rapidly. When water demand reaches 20%, water supply becomes an absolute limiting factor of economic development. It completely dominates economic planning.

Asia is already past the 20% mark; Europe and Africa will soon reach it as will parts of North America. The world toll is ten million deaths annually from waterborne intestinal diseases; over one third of the world's population lives in a state of debilitation due to impure water. Despite the limited nature of our water resources, nearly all of the 30,000 chemicals now in commercial production find their way into our water supplies. Each year another 1,000 compounds are added. (Some are lethal in even minute quantities, yet only 10% of them are tested for carcinogenity).

The relationship between resource use and economic viability, between short-term profits and long-term rewards, between gains in one part of the system and equal or greater losses in another have not been systematically recorded. No accurate accounting tools exist, there are no multi-dimensioned debit sheets currently employed that convey this information routinely.

But there have been chance recordings of these debits.

In Florida, manufacturers in the phosphate fertilizer industry found it good business to pollute neighbouring land with fluorine emissions from their smokestacks. Their profits were impeded, however, by lawsuits from their neighbours, who happened to be in the business of raising cattle. It seems the fluorine settled into the grasslands where the livestock grazed, giving the cattle fluorosis. The fluorosis stiffened the cattle's joints, immobilizing them so effectively that they starved to death. The courts decided that the livestock owners were in the right, and ordered the phosphate manufacturers to install pollution-control equipment.

The cost of eliminating 99% of the emissions (what the court required) came to $16 million, more than the phosphate manufacturers deemed it in their interest to pay. Rather than make an investment of this size—for which they'd get nothing in return—the manufacturers cleverly bought 200,000 surrounding acres at a cost of $25 million. (The court could not object to them polluting their own land.) This made them such large cattle owners that it paid them to install the equipment to protect their livestock investment.

Until you're in someone else's shoes, it's difficult to appreciate his problems. To the fertilizer manufacturers the livestock owners' concern about the factory's pollution seemed frivolous —the livestock owners weren't prepared to accept air pollution as a fact of life. Being forced to install pollution-control equipment, from the manufacturers' point of view, was contrary to free enterprise—a measure that would hold back economic growth. The phosphate company couldn't see that its growth was being made at someone else's expense, or that the economic growth of the area as a whole was being held back by its failure to install the pollution-control equipment.

Not until the fertilizer manufacturers found themselves in a position where they were paying for all the costs they were creating did they understand that it didn't make sense for one part of their operation to prosper at the expense of the other. They saw the relationship between conservation and economic growth.

Whether you see the trees or the forest, there are costs attached to every form of environmental degradation. The annual damage caused by air pollution in North America comes to about $22 billion (based on 1970 dollars). This is the known damage. The unknown damage can't be estimated because we don't yet know the extent of indirect damage triggered by air pollution, or when it will show up. The costs of cleaning it up would be about $23 billion. Looking just at these figures it doesn't seem to matter much either way whether we clean up the air or not—the costs of doing away with the damage just about equal the costs of the damage.

But as it happens, some industries do very little damage yet have to absorb the costs of damage caused by others. These relatively blameless industries pay in increased upkeep for their plants, lower property values, and sick pay for affected workers. This makes them less competitive than they might be, and puts them at a disadvantage in the marketplace. Meanwhile, other industries do a great deal of harm yet have to pay very little for it. These industries are artificially productive;

should they be forced to pay their own way, they would be vulnerable to economic collapse. With the growing strength of the environmental movement and the increasing use of the courts to protect private property from polluters, the probability is high that, sooner or later, the polluter will pay. (This principle has already been formally accepted and is being increasingly implemented by the members of the Organization for Economic Co-operation and Development, which includes Canada.) An industry that doesn't adapt and chooses to defy this probability could go the way of the dinosaur.

A breakdown of the various sectors of the economy (there are 41 categories, of which "households" is the only non-productive sector) shows that the brunt of the costs of air pollution are not always borne by those doing the polluting. Up to now the polluter does not always pay.

Only 5 of the 41 sectors do as much damage through air pollution as the costs to society-as-a-whole of cleaning it up. Assuming society is willing to pay the costs, we will break even. For 26 of the 41 sectors, the damage caused is much greater than the costs of cleaning it up. Here, it would pay society to foot the bill. In only 10 of the 41 sectors are the costs of clean-up much higher than the damages done. These ten sectors cause over 28% of the damage and one of them— households—accounts for more than 20% of the damage (mostly from its cars and furnaces). The other nine sectors combined account for about 8%.

Should society decide to make each sector pay its own way, most sectors (relative to the other sectors in our society) would be ahead when the final tally is worked out. The economy as a whole would be in a better position to promote growth, especially since its growth is being hampered by irresponsibility among households, which do not contribute directly to the economy's output.

Three sectors alone produce more than half of the environmental air damage: the utilities, the metal industry and households. Utilities cause 22.8% of the problem but would only be allocated 7.7% of the clean-up bill. The metal industries cause 11.8% of the damage but their bill to clean it up amounts to only 4.1% of the costs. The households cause 20.3% of the damage. To clean up their segment will cost 51.2% of the total clean-up bill.

If just these three segments could eliminate their share of air pollution—if air pollution could be reduced by 50%—it's estimated that the death rate would drop by 7%.

Besides being undesirable, death can be quite expensive. Few people arrange their demise to avoid for themselves (or society) costly medical bills, loss of income while in hospital, or financial inconvenience to their loved ones.

The costs of combatting environmental pollution are considerably lower than other costs concerned with public welfare such as health and education. Because the benefits are becoming so overwhelmingly clear to the OECD countries, their expenditures for fighting pollution have been increasing since 1971 and will, for most, reach about 2% of GNP.

The OECD expects that this across-the-board expense on environmental control measures among industrialized countries will help preserve the *status quo* in international trade. Since many of Canada's competitors will be paying about the same amount as Canada for pollution control, they'll have no trading advantage over us. As our pollution-plagued pulp and paper industry has already found out, we can set our shop in order without upsetting our export applecart.

The economic costs of living or working with pollutants are already staggering and could become unmanageable to industry. For the same reason that crewmen on a commercial freighter receive four times their regular pay for sailing through a war zone, workers whose jobs involve occupational hazards receive extra pay for their risk. This extra amount varies with the degree of risk, but continent-wide, it averages $360 per year for a job in which there's a one-in-a-thousand risk of dying in a year. Only one person in a thousand would die in a riskier job, but all thousand would receive the extra $360. The premium each company pays then, for a human life, averages $360,000.

Leaving aside the question of whether a human life is worth that much, the implications for growth in our economy are

ominous. The more industry pays out in unnecessary risk premiums, the less productive it tends to be. Historically, this
aspect of its productivity has been declining.

Industrialization in North America intensified around the
turn of the century when the spirit that produced the automobile and airplane helped the economy take off. At that time,
cancer deaths stood at 65 out of every thousand. Climbing
steadily with the climb of industrialization, the cancer rate rose
an average of about 1% per year, until 1975, when it rose 2%.
By 1975, the cancer death rate had risen to 171.5 per thousand,
and was costing $2 billion per year for hospital care, another
$5 billion for medical treatment and over $13 billion in lost
earning power and productivity. These $20 billion represent
the minutest fraction of cancer's cost to our economy. There's
an economic plague afoot, and it's so contagious it could set
the North American economy reeling.

Some 350,000 workers are exposed each year to one or more
trade-name substances that contain a carcinogen (cancer-caus-
ing chemical). But less than half of the work-place carcinogens
are identified to the potential victims. The actual number of
workers exposed to occupational risks of known carcinogens is
about one million. And cancer isn't the only disease arising out
of the workplace. Health authorities estimate that fully one
quarter of workers are exposed to substances that can cause
disease or death, and that 40% to 50% of all North Americans
may have been exposed to a recognized carcinogen or other
toxic substance in their working lifetimes.

Estimates of the number of deaths annually caused by occupation-related disease have been varied, and run high. A mod-
erate estimate is 150,000. Based on the current premium companies pay for human life, the direct corporate cost alone of
these 150,000 deaths could be $54 billion, or the equivalent of
another quadrupling of oil prices. Assuming workers do not
decide to value their lives more highly, and that the cancer rate
stops its historic climb, this is the sum the North American
economy could have to pay each year once occupational risks
become fully recognized.

It could be much cheaper to stop cancer and other occupational diseases than to allow these chemicals to cripple our economy.

About 6,000 new substances to which humans are exposed are developed each year (1,000 of them are used commercially). Reliable animal tests are time-consuming and average $150,000 each. The cost for testing all 6,000 (and most would not need testing) would come close to $1 billion—a bargain compared to the $54 billion annual fee we're facing.

But animal tests aren't always necessary. A new procedure, the Ames test, costs only $500 per substance and finds 90% of the carcinogens. Using this test to screen all the substances would cost about $3 million. Animal tests would still be necessary, but to a much smaller extent.

Cancer death rates vary from region to region, depending on the amount of pollution in each environment. If all of North America had the same rate as the most environmentally clean region has, the cancer mortality rate would drop by 90%. There's no reason we should allow the cancer rate to climb when the death rate for other diseases is on the decline. Cancer is controllable if we set a clean environment as a priority. If we don't, the economic progress we have been shakily constructing will be jeopardized by growing demands for compensation for risky work.

Ecological costs are real costs, but they are long-term costs. Because of this, they have been easy to ignore. Ultimately, they are translated into current economic costs and we may find the interest on those costs more than we're prepared to pay.

7 *Paying Our Way*

NO ONE LIKES to be known as a freeloader. Pity the poor executive caught failing to drop a quarter into the coin slot of a newspaper box or the secretary suspected of short-changing the office coffee pool. Accuse someone at work of not pulling his own weight and he'll quickly offer countless examples to the contrary. The accusation that someone is a freeloader carries the implication that someone else is picking up the tab. Of course, that's exactly the case.

Whether it's a wino on welfare or a corporate bum on a tax-deductible expense account, there's always outrage when others are seen as not paying their way. It's an inequity people instinctively abhor but not one that's always readily perceived.

Imagine that for some reason the government decided to pay for half the cost of all rugs purchased in Canada. It would lead to some people buying rugs instead of broadloom; others to buying two rugs when they might have bought one. Rugs would start adorning walls and become indispensable for patios. Given the economies of the situation, many might find it profitable to replace their rugs rather than going to the expense and bother of having them cleaned. Many more would realize that rugs make ideal and highly original gifts.

Although a boon to the rug-buyer, such a policy would be unfair for the person who likes wall-to-wall carpeting, and for the person whose floors don't need covering. Their tax

dollars would go to support reduced-priced rugs, which, because they're so generously supported, also become misused and overused. The multi-rug buyer pays taxes too, but unlike the rest of the population, his savings in rugs far exceeds the taxshare he puts in. Those who don't make a habit of buying rugs get nothing back for their share of tax dollars at all.

Because the idea of subsidizing rugs at the expense of broadloom is so absurd and unfair, governments have never done this. Instead they subsidize cars at the expense of public transit, nuclear energy at the expense of other forms of energy, and polluters at the expense of those who clean up after themselves.

Car owners pay for some of the services they use through taxes included in the price of gasoline. But most of the costs to the public—costs such as those associated with widening and repairing roads, salaries of traffic policemen, land taken out of public use to provide parking areas, increased hospital facilities to take care of accident victims and more courtrooms to take care of the victimizers—are paid for from general tax revenues, from car driver and non-driver alike.

These hidden subsidies make car-driving seem more economical than it in fact is, and lead many people to prefer cars to public transit. Because of the bargain, some buy two and even three cars. Many use cars when public transit would be as convenient.

If car owners were to pay their own way* (an additional tax of 70 cents per gallon would equal society's present subsidy to them), enormous sums of money would be freed for public use. One investment that would greatly benefit the car owners while being agreeable to other members of society would be to put these sums into an expansion of public transit, making it as comfortable and convenient as private transit.

With public transit a real option, many would leave their cars at home and commute by buses, streetcars and subways,

---

* Public transit is already subsidized, although to a much lesser extent than the automobile, and for very different reasons. Public transit is seen as a subsidy to businesses in its dual role of cheaply bringing workers and customers to them. Public transit is also seen as a necessity for those unable to afford the relative luxury of an automobile.

leaving the roads free of congestion for those whose individual preference remains the automobile. Merely by paying fully for their private decision to purchase a car (as, no doubt, most already think they are doing), all individuals in a conserver society could have added benefits from their transportation facilities. Travelling would not only be more enjoyable — travellers would also have more viable options to choose from.

Even when everyone uses a certain commodity — as in the case of electricity — many people are not paying their way. An individual who purchases a $20 electric space heater could be forcing society to spend as much as $2,000 to provide the electricity to meet the increased demand. Electricity used at peak periods costs the utility more to produce. The more units of electricity used, the more each additional unit costs. Also, each new plant that a utility builds tends to cost more than existing comparable plants.

In Ontario, for example, hydro-electricity, historically the first main source of power, still provides about 40% of the province's electricity at a cheap cost. The next 40% comes from various coal and oil-fired generators at many times the cost of hydro. The last 20% comes from nuclear generation. This costs even more than coal and oil-fired generators.

Instead of apportioning costs, so that an individual (or company) who uses cheaper electricity than another pays only at the cheaper rate, they both pay at an average rate that includes the high cost of new electricity (usually nuclear energy). No matter how much electricity someone saved, he'd by paying a rate that includes the cost of expensive electricity that wouldn't have been needed if others adopted his behaviour. Meanwhile, those with very high energy expenditures (for example, families that use many appliances) are being subsidized by those who get by with less electricity.

If people paid for electricity on the same basis that it costs the utility to produce the electricity, they would be able to pay their own way. Those who wished to take advantage of lower rates at various times could benefit directly from it (similar to low long-distance telephone rates on off hours). Those who didn't care what rate they paid could carry on as normal

(although their rates would probably also drop since less use by others would reduce overall use).

Paying your own way needn't be painful, as a large machine-shop operation in Kitchener, Ontario, discovered. It had the dirty habit of discharging its wastes into the city's sewage system. The wastes—oil-based cutting fluids—were so concentrated, though, that to satisfy the law, they first had to be diluted in great quantities of water. Although the machine shop didn't mind, the city fathers shuddered contemplating the plant's next expansion of business. To meet its civic responsibilities the city would have to invest in both a larger capacity water supply system and in a larger capacity sewage system. Progress for the plant was too pricey for the city.

When presented with this information, the machine shop chose not to threaten to relocate to a community that didn't care. Instead, the shop looked at alternatives, and found one at another firm located in the area. This firm developed a new technology which separated the oil from the waste. While the oil was reclaimed, the water was recycled. The new equipment to do this paid for itself in less than a year. By paying its own way, the machine shop not only prevented pollution, it picked up a profit in the process.

The industry with the least inclination to pay its own way is the packaging industry. A growth industry, its share of the costs of products for items as diverse as dairy products, beverages, and candy, has more than doubled over the last two decades. While total per capita consumption of food has increased 2.3% by weight the tonnage of food packaging has increased by 38.8%. The growth of the packaging industry can best be seen by picking through a garbage can or looking at the trash on the street near a fast-food outlet. Packaging now comprises more than half of all garbage, and to the taxpayer and municipal governments go the privilege of paying for the cost of its collection, waste handling, disposal and recycling. These costs are quickly accelerating. At the present rate, municipalities (even if they doubled their capacity to deal with garbage over the next decade) wouldn't be able to keep pace with the projected increase.

The stage is set for an historic political battle. Municipalities and the packaging industry are about to have a showdown over who will pay for the costs of the recycling that must take place. Until this battle is resolved, complete recycling of municipal wastes will not occur.

When a company decides not to pay its own way its costs spill over onto the balance sheet of others, so that its own balance sheet can show profits. This can be done by having costs forced on today's taxpayers (as with the social and environmental costs of cars and packaging) or on future generations (as with the German pharmaceutical firm that saved some testing costs and produced thalidomide). These profits are won at the expense of an unrecorded debit entry in some other part of our system.

Costs that aren't allocated properly mean that the resources that determine those costs won't be allocated properly. Poor allocation of resources destroys the free-market system, in which supply and demand are regulated by cost. It is this misallocation of resources that is sapping western economies and providing one of the thrusts for a conserver society. Since our western economies are based on the free-market system, our course is clear: to restore the free-market system we must restore the principle that everyone pays his own way.

Once this happens, we will be well on the way toward having a conserver society.

As much as anything else, a conserver society represents a new way of accounting, a way of accounting that recognizes total costs. Accepting these costs will represent the only added responsibility a conserver society will impose on any individual. It will insist we each pay our way.

The purchase price of many products usually includes most of the costs associated with them. Besides the production expenses the consumer pays for many indirect costs. Pollution abatement equipment sometimes raises the price of the product. An unclean environment in the workplace creates higher labour costs for the producer, both through higher wages when risky work is involved and through expensive sick pay when the work environment sickens employees. Pollution, whether from the producer's plant or from elsewhere, will increase his costs in upkeep, lower the value of his land, and cause his plant's value to depreciate. All these costs and more, which producers resolutely bear, are passed on to the consumer. Other costs are not passed on directly. Instead they're hidden in general taxes levied by the three levels of government. Costs associated with a product a person doesn't buy should not be paid by him, yet consumers end up paying these costs whether they helped cause them or not.

A more equitable way to account for costs would be to have all pollution costs paid for by the polluters, instead of partially by the polluters and partially by the taxpayer. Also, the costs of disposal and recycling could be paid for at the time of purchase, to ensure the owner assumes personal responsibility for the volume and type of garbage he produces. Having paid for all the costs associated with his purchase, including the costs of recycling, he will then be entitled to its value as a recyclable material.

In theory, the total cost for our economic system would be the same under both the existing and the conserver accounting systems. Instead of everyone paying similar amounts, those who use products that pollute more would pay more; those whose products polluted less would pay less. Instead of paying a garbage tax after disposal, disposal and recycling costs would be paid in advance. But overall, the costs to the system would add up to the same amount.

That's in theory. In practice a revolution in purchasing attitudes would take place. The end of the revolution would be marked by better-designed, lower-priced products across the board.

The direct costs of disposal are surprisingly low. Garbage collection comes to about a penny a pound. The extra amount a consumer would pay upon purchasing a one-pound pair of scissors would be one penny. A sofa that weighed 100 pounds would cost one dollar more when the disposal tax was added.

The value of recycled garbage can be high. Including the recycling tax paid at time of purchase, and the penny-a-pound collection cost, half a dozen all-aluminum cans would net the consumer about 25 cents for their value in aluminum. Despite what seems considerable expenses in garbage trucks, garbagemen, recycling plants, and administration costs, there's a significant profit to be made in the transaction. That 25 cent rebate could represent 20% of the cost of the cans and their contents, and it's kept after garbage collection costs have been met.

But add a second metal to the can, as happens when an aluminum top is placed on steel cans, and the situation is reversed. The combination makes the two metals difficult to recycle. The additional cost incurred could be as high as 20 cents a can, or $1.20 for a six-pack. Instead of getting back a quarter the person who purchases the same pop in aluminum-topped containers now loses 95 cents.

Often, it will be important to own a product that is difficult to recycle. In those cases, until a cheap method of resolving the problem comes about, purchasers will pay the necessary premium. But more often the difference between an easily recyclable and a hard-to-recycle product is negligible. When purchasing soft-drinks in a can most people neither know nor care what metal the top is made of. With the price differential a reflection of total costs, they'll come to care, and select those products designed most intelligently.

Garbage can have value through its retrievable components, and as fuel or compost. Which use garbage is put to will depend on advancements in recycling technologies. Garbage separated into various categories is presently much cheaper to recycle, and so those householders who decide to separate their garbage would be entitled to a larger credit. But most people separate their garbage already, although they're not always aware of it. People who use paper bags put their wet garbage elsewhere. Table scraps go into a garburator or a plastic bag. Old newspapers are usually stacked before disposal. For most people, separating garbage will involve no more than a six-inch movement of the hand.

Once a comprehensive recycling system is in place, computerized scales inside compartmentalized garbage trucks will instantly weigh, price and credit each home or building from which garbage is retrieved. Costs of operating this system would be infinitesimal compared to the costs of the rapidly escalating municipal solid wastes problem.

Meters installed on pipes leading to municipal sewage systems would allocate the value of liquid wastes generated by households. Putting value on garbage of all types would acknowledge the existence of the biosphere we live in, where all things interrelate and have some role to play in this living system.

A self-evident consequence of a society in which everything is recycled is that nothing stays as garbage. The goal of a pollution-free environment is neither technically unfeasible nor unlikely in practice.

The Kawasaki Corporation, on its own, decided to be a good corporate citizen and adopt a no-pollution policy. It did so with almost fanatic zeal. Spending 10-15% of its annual capital expenditure on pollution-control equipment, Kawasaki automatically recycles waste water from kitchens and purifies waste materials. Individual workers are responsible for making sure only paper goes into paper baskets and metal into scrap baskets. Sophisticated pollution-control systems such as oil separators that connect the factory drainage system to streams are labelled with the name of the man responsible for maintaining them in good order. Noise pollution is curbed too. Trucks driving past Kawasaki plants that don't slow down are noted and if the offending company has contracts with Kawasaki they're cancelled. In the plant, wooden chips are turned into solid blocks which are then machined into plant stands and sold to employees (adding $20,000 to corporate sales in the process).

These anti-pollution methods did not work to Kawasaki's disadvantage. Profits increased 16% and sales 19% after they were instituted.

Closer to home, McDonald's hamburger chain anticipated a recyclable economy and chose lightweight polystyrene packaging over virgin paper products. Polystyrene uses less energy in being produced, is a potentially profitable recyclable item (although not for food service uses because of sanitary factors) and if incinerated is an efficient source of energy.

Total recycling is a goal that is striven for at several Dow Chemical Company plants. Their general approach is to use the wastes from one process as the raw materials for another. Salt wastes, for example, from the production of mining chemicals are conditioned and used in another process. Similarly, a dilute acid waste stream from chlorination units is converted for use elsewhere in the plant.

Du Pont is another company interested in the total recycling concept. It has developed a cell less than one cubic foot in volume that removes up to 90% of the copper from a 100-gallon-per-minute waste stream containing 5-100 parts per million. Du Pont points out that to salvage more of the copper (it presently achieves only 99.99999% purity) two cells can be used or the speed of the waste stream can be reduced.

Du Pont is currently working on the development of similar cells for other metals, but machinery will not be needed to recycle the last microscopic iota of mineral to achieve a 100% rating. Animal life depends on minute concentrations of minerals and plants require quite substantial mineral concentrations. Trace elements released into the air find their way into the water table and then into the systems of plants and animals, fulfilling biological needs.

The mineral absorption characteristic of plants is so great that they may replace machines in recycling minerals, or even in mining them. Vital minerals such as potassium, calcium, manganese, nitrogen, phosphorus, sulphur, chlorine and silicon are already mined routinely by plants, then concentrated and stored conveniently in their root systems. Minerals constitute 5% of the dry weight of plants, concentrating five billion metric tons of minerals each year or five times the production of human endeavours in mining operations.

Paying our way will free our economy from many of its artifical constraints and free it to develop in more natural directions.* But a fundamental natural constraint remains—

* In a study by Chase Econometrics (a division of The Chase Manhattan Bank) for the U.S. Government, the effect on the economy of moving towards a pollution-free environment was beneficial. It would lead to a higher growth rate and a greater increase in GNP than the increase that could be expected if environmental standards were not met.

perhaps the best publicized yet least understood economic dilemma of the decade: how to assure an adequate energy supply in an energy-dependent world.

8 Conservation and Unlimited Economic Growth

II—Energy

A BILLION BARRELS of oil saved is a billion barrels of oil earned. Energy gained through conservation is just as valuable as energy gained from finding a new oil well or building a new generating station. It will run as many automobiles, heat as many homes, light up as many lightbulbs. But it won't cost as much.

It would cost $6.3 billion to insulate every home in Canada to a moderate level. In terms of the energy that saves over the life of the house, the cost is exceedingly small—less than one tenth the cost of the extra fuel that would have been needed in the case of a gas- or oil-heated home and one twentieth the cost of providing that heat from nuclear energy.

Because we're running out of fossil fuels, enormous investments are being made trying to find more. Oil and gas from our Arctic, the North Sea and North America's outer continental shelf require between $10,000 and $15,000 for each barrel's worth of energy provided per day.

Synthetic gas and oil, produced from coal, require even more capital, probably about twice as much as Arctic gas and oil for an equivalent amount of delivered energy.

Coal is relatively cheap as a direct energy source—about one third the cost of oil and gas for new supplies—but it is neither as flexible as oil and gas nor as dependable a source. Environmental and safety problems in coal mining, processing and combustion have limited the rate of coal consumption and will raise the cost of supply.

The production of electrical energy requires a much greater capital investment than fossil fuels—14 times that of oil and gas when the electricity is produced from coal; 23 times when it is produced from a nuclear source such as uranium.

Canada is already experiencing a severe capital crunch, with investment dollars harder and harder to find. But our capital requirement of $24.5 billion in 1976 seems modest compared to the estimates of $700 billion needed from now to 1985.

While business is scrambling for its share of capital—capital it needs for continued growth—our massive energy needs are pre-empting it, creating increasing stresses in capital markets. Before the oil crisis in 1973, our investment in the supply and distribution of energy equalled 25% of all business investment. The fears over our fuel supplies (reinforced by the world recession the oil crisis triggered) are pushing the share of investment dollars going to energy needs to almost 50%. This has squeezed the capital available for the rest of the business sector. The shortage is so severe it threatens our entire economy.

The situation is no less serious in the United States. Over the next decade close to half of all American business investment will be required by the energy sector. The balance of business and industry will go begging. Money to get the goods out won't be available—it will be tied up in making the energy to make the goods. A complete collapse of the North American economy is far from being in the realm of fantasy.

For an economy to run smoothly, it should have as much energy as it needs. If it doesn't, it will run at three-quarter speed or one-half speed, or whatever rate the energy supply allows. Because an adequate energy supply is an absolute necessity, such staggering sums are being siphoned out of traditional investments into the production of energy. It's a desperate drive to raise our energy supplies to match our energy demands.

A far easier solution would be to lower our energy demands to meet our energy supplies. A car that travels 1,000 miles on 50 gallons of gas travels just as far as a car that travels 1,000 miles on 100 gallons of gas. An economy that can sustain a steady growth in GNP based on conservation of energy can grow just as much as an economy that bases its growth on finding new energy supplies.

And it can keep on growing for many decades. Such an economy won't be strangled by a shortage of capital, won't be subject to blackmail when a few sheiks on the other side of the world get upset, and won't have to hold its breath while oil rigs probe the bottom of the seas looking for enough fuel to bail it out once more.

The potential for conservation is impressive. In an ideal system, all of our energy would be used to 100% efficiency; there would be no waste. We aren't about to approach 100% efficiency even looking far, far into the future. We aren't destined to remain at close to 100% waste either.

We have been used to measuring energy efficiency by how completely a fuel is consumed in accomplishing its task. By this standard, a home furnace that achieves a 60% or 70% efficiency rating in burning oil is not unusual. But different forms of energy are suited to different tasks. Despite its high capital cost, electricity is indispensible for many of our energy needs. It's such a high-grade fuel that electricity is often cheaper and more efficient than other forms of energy. A gas-powered clock would not make economic sense. Neither would a coal-fired television. Conversely, it's inefficient to use electricity for low-grade energy needs, such as home heating. It will do the job, but then caviar could substitute for rock salt in de-icing your driveway.

Electricity can heat to very high temperatures. If we wanted our homes kept at a comfortable 500°, an electrical heating system might make sense. At current comfort levels, however, using electricity for heat at 20°C means that energy available at excruciatingly high temperatures must first be cooled down —a somewhat inefficient procedure. Solar energy is more efficient. It arrives at a temperature a house can tolerate.

Different energy forms are appropriate for different energy uses, and the better we can match appropriate energy supplies to satisfying those uses the better our efficiency. Using this yardstick to measure efficiency, the furnace that appears to be 60% or 70% efficient is more likely only about 6% efficient. Other energy efficiencies become equally unimpressive.

The average efficiency of Canadians in heating water is 3%—the other 97% of the energy we assign to this task is wasted in the effort. When heating our homes and offices, the efficiency doubles to 6%. It's 5% for air conditioning and refrigeration; 10% when running an automobile, 21% for producing·steel, 9% when refining petroleum, 10% in the manufacture of cement and less than 1% in producing paper.

The fuel used in all these areas combined accounts for about 60% of our entire energy bill. The average efficiency of all the fuel used in these areas (and the average efficiency of all the fuel used in our economy) is 8.3%. The amount wasted, the reservoir from which we could draw with sensible conservation measures is 91.7%. Even a small portion of that 91.7% would solve our current and future energy problems. With only a modest reduction in waste of only 1%—from 91.7% to 90.7%—we would save the energy equivalent of close to half a million barrels of oil per day—more than enough to compensate for all the oil Canada imports.

Conservation means more than flicking off the lights and filling our attics with fibreglass insulation. The idea of matching energy supplies to energy needs is only common sense and implies no hardship. It doesn't mean scrimping on the energy we use; it means scrimping on the energy we don't use.

Too much of our potentially available energy eludes us. Industrial process steam, for example, accounts for about 40% of industrial energy and about 15% of the nation's energy. It can be produced directly from a boiler, which means that the boiler's ability to heat water to several thousand degrees under high pressure produces only steam at a temperature of several hundred degrees under low pressure. Or it can be produced as a by-product of electrical production. That same boiler, producing high-pressure steam can first turn turbines to generate electricity. When the steam has done this job, it's still available for industry as process steam.

In many European countries, this concept, called co-generation, already produces close to 30% of all electricity. North America uses it to produce only 5% to 10% of the electricity, despite its proven technology and enormous potential. In just three industries—paper-making, chemicals and petroleum refining—we have the opportunity to produce over one-third of all our continent's electrical needs through co-generation and the recovery of some of the waste heat.

Conservation can often have immediate effects at low capital cost, both to individuals and to industry. An example can be seen by looking at the cost and energy efficiencies of the common air conditioner. By paying an extra $45, you can buy an air conditioner that is 89% more efficient in providing the same 5,000-BTU-per-hour cooling capacity. Based on an average use of 500 hours per year, the energy saving to you is about $20 per year.

The saving to society is much greater. Assuming the air conditioner is used on hot summer days, when demand is high and electricity costly to the utility, the $45 paid for conservation has a value of over $200 per year.

By paying our own way, this saving should be passed on to the individual. Instead of charging an average price for electricity, our utilities could charge more for peak-load hours and peak-load seasons and less when demand falls off. For the individual who carries on as normal, the utility bill would stay about the same. For those who decide to take advantage of simple measures such as using efficient air conditioners the savings are sizeable. In the case of the air conditioner, the annual saving is more than its original retail selling price.

Industry could make similar savings by paying its own way on its utility bills and on its own energy-generating equipment. Waste-heat recuperators can provide savings of at least 25% on most high-temperature furnaces used for certain types of metal processing. They pay for themselves in three to four years. Waste heat can also be used to generate electricity. An engineering study conducted for a major cement manufacturer showed that a $2.7 million system could recapture enough waste heat to produce a capacity of 4,700 kilowatts of electricity.

The cement company decided against installing the system although it would have saved $775,000 per year, paying for the $2.7 million investment in only three and a half years. The company just didn't have the capital to invest in conservation. Lack of capital also prevents metal processors from installing waste-heat recuperators.

Capital is so scarce that companies would rather save it for preferred business purposes such as tooling new products and expansion of capacity. The major reason it's so scarce, of course, is that utilities are draining capital markets to fund their expensive energy-finding projects.

But for those same utilities, the cost of producing energy through conservation measures is much lower. A waste-heat recuperator represents a capital investment for fuel saved that's one fourth the cost of supplying new gas. The cement company's electricity from waste heat would have cost one half to one third of the average investment required for new electrical sources.

Conservation has become this economical because all the cheap sources of energy have already been tapped. New sources are prohibitively priced. It costs Hydro-Quebec $12,000 in new investment, for example, for every new electrically heated home that's built in the suburbs. If a small part of that investment were made for conservation a great part would not need to be spent at all.

To raise the capital needed for conservation, our publicly owned utilities could lend some of their money to industry and to individuals for conservation purposes. Rather than put money into off-shore drilling it could be more efficiently invested at home. The customers who borrow for conservation would have lower energy bills. This would allow them to pay their normal utility rate while paying off the debt (with interest) without feeling the strain. After several years, when the debt was paid off, they would get to keep the fuel savings for themselves. The utility, meanwhile, would have earned interest on its loan and spent less to gain the same amount of energy.

The potential for energy conservation lies everywhere, and any one of a number of combinations can produce even a growth-oriented economy without massive demands on scarce capital. One ten-year plan designed for the United States by Elias P. Gyftopoulos of MIT and Thomas F. Widmer of the Thermo Electron Corporation, two of the United States' most relied upon energy experts, would allocate $61 billion for new supplies of energy and $157 billion for conservation—a total of $218 billion. This would allow a real growth in GNP of 3% per year while bringing energy consumption back to 1975 levels. None of the plan's measures require unproven technology.

Without courting economic collapse, this conservation plan would cost about one quarter of the cost of financing an equal growth without conservation. The net effect of its implementation would be to raise the average efficiency of energy use from the present 8.3% to 10.9%—a paltry 2.6%—over a 10-year period.

This is only the beginning for conservation. To maintain an average growth in GNP of 3% per year would require an increase in efficiency of only one percentage point every two and a half years. No increase in energy use would be needed. Even then, at this modest rate, by the year 2015 our across-the-board average efficiency would be only 20%, about equal to that of the steelmaking process today.

Such an achievement would be neither remarkable nor unparalleled. The efficiency of electric generating plants rose steadily for a comparable number of decades at a higher rate. Because these plants have been subjected to enormous and continuing commitments of technological resources—the same prescription needed for energy conservation measures—their efficiency is now in excess of 40%.

At the beginning of this decade, Canada's Minister of Energy estimated we had enough oil to pull us through the next 392 years. The estimate was revised downward by some 380-odd years just three years later, and we soon began importing oil.

Besides being embarrassing, there are serious consequences when an economy must depend on unknown or unstable supplies of energy. Changeovers are disruptive and costly. The basis for economic growth becomes a roulette wheel.

With the same certainty that William Stanley Jevons, at the

peak of the Industrial Revolution, predicted its end based on the lack of availability of coal, it's clear that the present industrial era based on abundant fossil fuels is drawing to a close. Our present economy is as unsustainable, as vulnerable to violent ruptures as the era of the Industrial Revolution, as long as it's based on resources that will run out.

Unlike non-renewable fuels, conservation is forever. Its savings will provide the equivalent of the fuel we'll need for the foreseeable future, but it isn't the entire answer. Ultimately, our economy may need more energy than this kind of conservation can provide. It may need the conservation of different sources of energy, sources that won't run out.

Those sources are available today. They are known by the blanket term of renewable energy, and include solar energy, wind power, hydro-electricity, and a host of other energy forms. One way or another, they all get their energy from the sun.

We are well accustomed to conserving the energy in falling water by converting it to electricity. Not damming up a suitable river seems to many a shameful waste of an available resource. We are less accustomed to conserving the energy in moving air, or in the rays of the sun that bounce off our buildings. Yet this energy—left untapped—is lost to us. Tapped, it could provide a basis for uninterrupted, unlimited, economic growth. The sun provides the earth with virtually all its energy. We could never do better than learn how to harness it.

Communities based on hydro-electric power are nothing new. Solar communities and wind-powered communities have already been built, and soon they'll be nothing new. The advantage of renewable energy sources however, besides their dependability, is that they can be decentralized—used even on individual bases. This could be a basis for individual freedom —one less area in which we're obliged to say grace to the State. Rather than depend on transmission lines from utilities that have enriched our language with brownouts and blackouts, our power supplies can be our own. To the individual, renewable sources of energy can mean not worrying about water pipes freezing during an extended power interruption, or not shivering, or not having to throw out the food in the freezer after an unscheduled thaw. Industry could depend on uninterrupted production from secure supplies. Fear of blackouts has already induced many companies to purchase costly back-up generators. To society a conversion to renewable energy sources will mean that whatever form of economic progress it chooses will be on a firm footing, dependent for its energy merely on the sun's rising each morning.

But before the Canadian economy can progress, the peculiarly Canadian problem of why we have been unable to establish a manufacturing base—despite huge inputs into our research and development capabilities—will have to be resolved.

PART THREE

Discovering What We Want

9   *The Research Discovery*

AFGHANISTAN DOESN'T DO very much research; it also doesn't produce very much and has, by our standards, a low standard of living. This is reflected in its Gross National Product. The United States, in contrast, does a great deal of research. It also has a high level of production and, as a result, what's commonly considered an uncommonly high standard of living. Its GNP is the highest in the world. In between Afghanistan and the United States are a lot of other countries, including Canada, doing varying amounts of research and having varying standards of living.

For an industrialized nation or for an industry, technological innovation is an indispensable component—as vital to success as manpower or capital. More than half of all world economic growth is attributed to technological innovation. This innovation can come by way of productivity gains, through new contributions to existing industries, or through the creation of completely new industries. For industrialized countries, 30% to 50% of long-term economic growth stems from innovation which improves productivity, and another 30% to 50% from innovations which lead to new products, processes, or completely new industries.

Of the 100 largest American companies at the close of the Second World War, most have lost their ranking. Their places have been taken up by companies which either didn't exist then or were insignificant in size if they did. The newcomers owe their present position not to financial wizardry but to new technologies, new processes, and new products. They owe their growth to innovation.

You don't have to be big to become the best, even in a country dominated by big business. Although 80% of industrial research and development money may be spent by 200 large corporations (as in the United States) or by three or four industries (as in Canada) more than two thirds of the basic discoveries that resulted in important innovations came from independent inventors or small firms. The FM radio, the mercury dry cell, the dry electrostatic copier, penicillin, streptomycin and insulin, the modern rocket engine, the zipper, the self-winding watch, instant photography and air conditioning all came from individuals not working for large companies.

Most technological innovations are based on well-known scientific and technical knowledge—they do not depend on sophisticated scientific discoveries. By implication, small Canadian companies and independent Canadian inventors should be at no disadvantage. Unlike other countries, though, Canada offers no financial incentives for the independent to innovate, and doesn't help small companies market their innovations. As a result what inventions we have are commonly sold to large concerns for development, usually large American concerns.

Canadians are no dummies. With so much evidence showing that research and development have a direct relationship to productivity and economic growth, logic might have been expected to dictate a simple course: increase the funding for research and development. Yet the Canadian economy has done the reverse.

Canada now spends only 1% of its GNP on research and development—half the science budget of industrialized countries in Europe of comparable size, 40% as much as the United States. Our industry spends one-third to one-half of what industry in other countries spends on research and development, and performs only 30% of the national research effort compared to 60% for France, West Germany, and the Netherlands. The combined research effort of Canadian-owned corporations in mining and metallurgy, pulp and paper, telecommunications, steel, and food technologies—areas where we are among the largest in the world—generally amounts to less than 1% of sales.

Only 3 of 12 Canadian multi-nationals employ more than 100 qualified scientists and engineers in research and development. There are only 13 independent laboratories employing more than 100 qualified scientists and engineers. Of 1000 independent research establishments, three quarters employ fewer than five scientists—the minimum level generally considered necessary for effective research.

Only a decade ago, in 1967, Canada's standing in the world research community seemed acceptable. The United States and the United Kingdom put much more emphasis on technological advancement. But France, Germany, Japan, the Netherlands and Sweden all had research efforts similar to Canada's, and the efforts of Italy, Belgium, and Norway were considerably below those of Canada's. We seemed to be in an average position among the other industrialized countries—not surprising as our position in overall production was also average.

But surprisingly, Canada ranked last among ten western industrialized countries in technological innovation, according to an international report published in 1969. The report established 110 significant innovations since World War II and found that none of them was first practised in Canada.

Ironically, it was during this same period the report covered that Canadian industry was increasing its involvement in research and development. Starting in the early 1960s, new research laboratories—spurred on by government incentive schemes—opened in many countries which previously hadn't had any. This accelerated to a peak in 1965, when a new lab opened every six days. Growth continued until the optimism of Canada's centennial year faded away in 1968 or 1969. We have been sliding downhill ever since.

Many of the smaller labs closed shop. Some of the giants of Canadian industry slashed their research budgets severely. Others closed their laboratories altogether. Industry discovered that research and development in Canada doesn't pay, that the present structure of industry forecloses its future so effectively that no amount of research and development could make it competitive. Rather than investing its profits in future growth that wasn't materializing, industry pocketed its profits instead.

The factors stunting our research and development efforts all stem from one root: Canadian industry is foreign-controlled. Ours is a branch-plant economy in which most of the fruits of our research and development efforts flow away from Canada.

One factor involves the size of the Canadian market. Although it is comparable to most European countries, it is dwarfed by the American market which, because of the economies of scale, can produce goods at lower costs. A Canadian manufacturer competing with an American manufacturer is likely to be the loser. His costs will be higher. If the Canadian manufacturer has a new product to market, however, there is no direct competition from any foreign manufacturer. With this advantage, the Canadian would have the market to himself until others could duplicate his product. In the interim, the Canadian, having a head start, would have the opportunity to refine the product and create another new market.

This is the characteristic way technological changes are introduced: rapid obsolescence results from successive generations of improvements, with the benefits usually accruing to the original innovator. For this reason, all else being equal, there is no correlation between the size of a national market and technological innovation. It is only after innovation stops and a product matures that the advantage gravitates to the country with the greater market.

All else is not equal in Canada. Many of our corporations are subsidiaries of foreign corporations, mostly American corporations. This is an advantage in that the free flow of information between them gives us access to an immense amount of foreign research and development—as much as fifty times what we generate.

But it's a disadvantage in that it gives the parent company access to the Canadian subsidiary's discoveries. Because of the ultimate economies of scale, because the most experienced and generally most competent teams of engineering and marketing people in multinational corporations are found in the parent country, because the general level of engineering and development in Canada is low and because a new manufacturing plant often has to be built in Canada while an existing one in the parent country is already in place, it will be cheaper for the multinational to manufacture in the country with the larger market or in its home country. That country will not usually be Canada.

Although the company could be manufacturing the product in Canada and making a profit, the profit would not be as great as that from a product manufactured in the foreign country. The decision by the company is rational. It acts in its own best interests. Those interests just don't happen to coincide with Canada's. Nor do they leave much elbow-room for Canadian-owned innovation to assert itself.

Foreign ownership is low in backward industries with below-average growth rates. It is concentrated in the research-intensive industries and through them it dominates their research and development activities. In effect, it dominates research and development in Canadian industry. As long as this remains the case, as long as Canadian research and development activities act as a subsidy to foreign industry—mostly in the United States—Canada's position cannot improve.

Canada's position is unique in the world. No other industrialized country permits such extensive ownership of its industry (67%) to lie outside its borders (and largely outside its control). No other industrialized country becomes progressively worse as an exporter of manufactured goods.

Foreign ownership in Canada cannot be scoffed at any longer. But "Buying Back Canada" policies would do little to redress the problem, since the foreign-based firms are often not worth buying. Their value is not in their function as manufacturers but in their being a means of exporting to Canada. Many do little or no manufacturing at all. They import from their parent companies to sell to the Canadian market. They can do this more cheaply than Canadian companies because they don't face the same overheads—little more than a sales office will do for them while a Canadian company has to set up entire manufacturing capabilities. The administrative superstructure has already been set up in the United States; the Canadian subsidiary is merely plugged into it.

Also, marketing is much easier for the American firm. Not only does it have the enormous expertise that comes with size, but much of the advertising paid for in the United States spills across the border to become a free advantage for the subsidiary in Canada. The Canadian firm is hardly on an equal footing.

Discriminatory legislation against existing foreign ownership (although the practice of allowing further foreign control could be curtailed outright) is not necessarily the answer. A more equitable solution would be to set non-discriminatory standards affecting all companies and reflecting Canadian needs. As legitimate expressions of national policy, they would not invite retaliation.

In the United States, such an expression might have been its exploration of space. In Great Britain, it was the decision to join the European Common Market. In France, it is a national commitment to develop the country's defense capabilities. For Canada it could be the adoption of a conserver society.

Almost as if some grand design were at work, the standards that would be set by a conserver society, and the directions its research would take, could assure that technological innovation and its benefits would benefit Canadians.

10 *Directions for Research*

IT'S TOO LATE for Canada to contemplate being the first to land a man on Mars. No matter how hard we'd try, it would be a practical impossibility to overcome the technological lead the United States has built up in space travel. Creating a computer competitive with IBM's is equally out of this world. IBM may not have NASA's lead but its advantage is nevertheless overwhelming. In the research race, the first competitor out of the gate is usually the winner. A late starter can overtake the leader—as the United States overtook Russia in the space race—but such an achievement requires a massive commitment. More often the leader hangs onto the lead.

The idea is to get into the lead. To get into the lead, it helps to know where you're heading.

Canada, and the rest of the world, is heading inevitably towards a conserver society. Only the date and means of arrival are yet to be determined—almost all agree that eventually our resources would otherwise run out. Faced with this inevitability, most of the world's research efforts are directed towards resisting the inevitable. Virtually all research into the use of our natural resources is aimed at finding and developing better extraction and processing methods—relatively little goes into developing recycling technologies. Virtually all research into meeting our energy needs is aimed at producing more non-renewable energy. Relatively little goes into developing renewable energy sources and conservation.

At this juncture in history, Canada has the opportunity to seize the initiative and accept the inevitable.

Nothing is as compellingly inevitable as the need for conservation and renewable energy sources. Yet despite their irresistability, by the end of the next decade only 3% of our energy is scheduled to come from renewables. Most of our energy is still slated to come from our conventional sources, sources we'll be spending hundreds of billions of dollars to develop. Conservation methods alone can eliminate most of the need to develop further insecure sources. The relatively modest amount of $6.3 billion spent in conservation can keep every home in Canada just as warm in the winter and cool in summer as it is now while using half as much energy.

Those who've dared conserve energy have been rewarded for their courage. Carleton University invested less than $20,000 over a three-year period and now saves almost $600,000 per year on its energy bill. The savings of the smaller McMaster University's Medical Centre are on a larger scale—$2,222,000 after four years of conserving. The Federal Government's savings from all of its energy conservation efforts in 1977 totalled $30 million, or enough energy to heat 50,000 homes. One building alone—headquarters for the External Affairs Department—has cut back its fuel consumption to almost one third of what it used when it first opened in 1973. Savings to business and industry are no less substantial. A single hotel—the Sheraton Centre in Toronto—saves $200,000 per year by operating a computerized energy control system.

To achieve most of these savings, little more was done than put in storm windows and turn off air conditioners on cool days. One company, Dominion Foundries and Steel of Hamilton, Ontario, simply switches off main office lights overnight and on weekends for its $75,000 annual savings.

There's no cause to feel smug saving such sums through conservation methods of these kinds. Instead of the 25% to 50% fuel savings these organizations have achieved they could be aiming for 80% or 90%. The potential is there. If buildings were better designed, if they used materials that had better insulating qualities, if there were thermostats in every room and simple devices to watch them, and simple devices to watch furnaces, and simple devices to watch water heaters, cutting back by 80% or 90% would be routine.

It isn't routine because it doesn't always pay to conserve to those standards. Research is needed to make it pay.

Solar heating is in its infancy. In 1976 there were fewer than twenty private and publicly sponsored solar projects and buildings in Canada. Two years later, there were more than 200. Within another ten years, the number of homes using solar energy could approach two million. By then, with the price of conventional fuels having gone up while solar energy costs have come down, solar heating would be preferred for all new buildings, either to assist in heating (for buildings having large heating requirements) or to fully satisfy heating needs. Only buildings that don't have access to the sun or have access to unusually low-cost alternate heating would fail to capitalize on the free benefits of solar energy.

Although solar could be the most significant growth industry since the computer, our present investment in solar technologies is minimal. The first generation of solar collector (the flat plate solar collector) is only beginning to be supplanted by a second generation (the evacuated-tube solar collector). There will be third- and fourth-generation collectors; there will be more effective ways of storing solar energy; there will be more efficient ways to convert solar energy to electricity. Unless Canada vigorously enters the field, these innovations will be born elsewhere and won't benefit us.

Using biomass—harnessing the power in wood, wastes, and other organic material—may be an approach of even greater potential for Canada. If solar energy is in its infancy, biomass has barely been conceived. Its value lies in its versatility. Biomass promises to satisfy many of our specific energy needs: converted to liquid fuels it can run our cars; converted to gaseous fuels it can be used for heating; converted to electricity it can run our electric appliances.

Biomass energy can be obtained almost anywhere, from almost anything, even from sources that are presently neglected. Pulp-and-paper-mill wastes, brushwood, and all types of low-grade standing timber can be converted to energy. A ton of green wood, for example, has the energy content of about 6,500 cubic feet of natural gas, or a third of a ton of coal. In a country where much of our agricultural land is marginal at best, farms that wouldn't be profitable producing low-yield food crops could be utilized successfully producing high-yield energy crops.

Electricity is the most expensive form of energy in commercial use. In the United States, NASA estimates that wind power can provide up to 10% of the nation's entire electrical needs. In Canada, wind power could be an even greater factor in making us self-sufficient in electricity. Because our population is so dispersed, costly and inefficient transmission lines connect communities far from the power source. These communities are vulnerable to blackouts and brownouts caused hundreds of miles away, and dependent upon repair crews reaching isolated areas.

Wind power would eliminate this dependance and save energy and money for utilities. Many areas of Canada have enough wind year-round to provide the majority of their electrical needs. The eastern coasts of Nova Scotia, Newfoundland and Labrador, the western coast of Hudson Bay, the St. Lawrence Basin, southern Saskatchewan, and most of Alberta could be generating electricity from wind.

Nor does the potential for wind power stop there. Windmills could be hooked into the national energy grid to provide electricity for general use or they could be placed on city rooftops to meet specific needs. When we learn how to store electricity efficiently, so that power generated when the wind is strong can be used when it's not, the windmill's untold possibilities will unfold.

Windmills can be large or small, sleek or stocky. Their cost can be remarkably low and their applications remarkably varied. But since they went out of vogue a half-century ago, their development as an energy source has been almost entirely ignored.

Despite the backward state of the art, wind power makes so much sense an American town has already been converted to it. In Canada, while some experimentation is going on (most notably a vertical-axis windmill developed by the National Research Council) we have yet to tell in what direction the wind's blowing. Research funding for wind energy remains minimal.

Canadian research should aim at developing renewable energy technologies: solar, biomass, wind, tidal power, and a host of others. At the moment an infinitesimal portion of our total energy research dollars goes here. Instead, most of our energy efforts are directed toward developing more fossil fuels and nuclear power. Our nuclear power technology is one of the most successful on earth.

Canada joined the research race for peaceful uses of nuclear energy shortly after the war. Because the development became a national commitment, because no country had an overwhelming lead in technology, and because we developed reactors to suit Canadian needs, our CANDU now stands as the most efficient nuclear reactor in the world. Despite intense competition from other countries, it has unique characteristics that make it competitive in world markets.

The CANDU reactor is an example of what Canadian research can do; but it's an unfortunate example. The CANDU is only the best of a bad lot. Nuclear energy is suspect on too many grounds for it to become acceptable when viable alternatives exist. Its total costs are far in excess of other forms of energy, the ramifications of a nuclear accident are so overwhelming no insurance company will take the risk of offering protection against it, no safe disposal method exists for the nuclear wastes, and the plutonium in those wastes can become A-bomb material for anti-social terrorists and once-friendly governments. In any event, nuclear energy is seen as only a short-term solution. Nuclear plants are built to last 30 years, or about as long as our government expects our uranium reserves to last. At that point the plants themselves, having become dangerously radioactive, will have to be disposed of along with the other nuclear wastes.

Until these possibly insoluble nuclear questions are resolved, continuing an intense program of nuclear development will not provide an adequate rate of return for the investment. Instead, funds could be shifted to those areas likely to reward the effort. Although it may be difficult to walk away from a research effort spanning more than three decades, it's also unwise to keep throwing good money after bad. If research and development into nuclear energy is to continue, it should do so at a rate that its potential can justify, and not at the expense of projects far likelier to meet national objectives.

A conserver society would run on renewable energy and be built of recycled materials. As a direct consequence of recycling our materials, we would be reducing pollution while saving energy and retaining use of the materials. Pollution control, energy, and materials are all in great demand. The benefits are so sweeping that research into these areas can't help but be rewarded.

The recycling that presently takes place uses a fraction of the technology a conserver society would demand. Because the entire world still depends on conventional sources for the supply of natural resources, a Canadian commitment towards a 100% recycling technology would stand apart from any other country's. It would establish us as undisputed leaders in this field and result in Canadian stewardship over an approaching world-wide industry.

One way to reduce waste is by recycling. Throwing away a pound of copper when it can be recycled and used again is not efficient. Another way to reduce waste is by doing more with less. If a half-pound of copper can be made to do the same job, why use a pound?

The ability to do more with less—the result of synergy—denies there's an absolute limit to growth. Before the discovery of this principle, it was fashionable to believe that there was a limit to how many people the earth could sustain. Because there was only so much land (and other resources) that could produce the food (and other requirements) needed for life, the belief was that eventually we would run out of resources. This created the fuss over the population explosion, and also led to inward-looking philosophies dooming a growth-oriented society. What the originator of this philosophy—Thomas Malthus

—failed to anticipate more than a century ago was the unpredictable result of the union of two or more predictable commodities. He failed to anticipate synergetic relationships.

Steel, for example, is the synergetic result of the union of iron and coke. Knowing the physical properties of iron and coke would not have been sufficient to predict the physical properties of steel. Because of synergy, farmland can yield five and ten times what it used to, a million telephone conversations can be sent along a single wire and synthetic rubber can indefinitely stretch supplies from rubber tree plantations. Natural resources can be used with ever-increasing efficiency. The absolute limiting factor on mankind's growth becomes not the physical resources of the earth but the psychic resources of the human mind in using those physical resources. We can grow, perhaps infinitely, as long as our growth doesn't exceed the rate at which we learn to use our resources.

It is within this joint framework that a conserver society must function. Technological growth is no alien to a conserver's world, but it must know its place in that world.

Because of the importance of technology to a conserver society, a direction for Canadian research is in the technology with the greatest potential for doing more with less—electronics. We have too little knowledge of the digital computer to enter that field but the micro-computer was only invented in 1970, and many of its applications have yet to be appreciated. By concentrating our efforts on those applications particularly relevant to Canada we could build our store of knowledge without competing with other countries for the same information. Once the knowledge is applied we'll have products relevant to our needs and—almost certainly—to the needs of others as well.

Canada was able to successfully develop the CANDU nuclear reactor because—alone of all the countries—we built our reactor to run on uranium that didn't need to be enriched. We could do this because the uranium needed for our reactor is abundant here—the CANDU was designed specifically with Canadian needs in mind. Designing a product to specific criteria gives it purpose while eliminating competition for the same set of knowledge. The unique result often finds applications in foreign markets.

The second generation solar collector differs from the first in several respects. One of them is that the second generation collector is more efficient at lower temperatures. This makes it more relevant to Canadian needs than the first, but not as relevant as it could have been had it been designed specifically for the Canadian climate.

This is the challenge for Canadian research and its advantage. The United States might inadvertently design a collector that's best for our needs. The collector we would design would specifically meet those needs.

Necessity will often mother our cold-weather innovations. Transportation is one major concern. The Turbo train had trouble for years because it was designed for the American South. Toronto's much-heralded elevated public transit monorail of the mid-seventies—the Skytrain—never got off the ground because its German designers didn't appreciate the consequences of ice forming on tracks. The Turbo's problems were resolved; the Skytrain's were not. Both cost too much money in the process.

Canadian firms conscious of Canadian needs could have done better. Many climate-related technologies need development for our North. The Canadian Arctic will need the development of permafrost technologies. Facilities for tourists in the North need study. Most of our untapped hydro-generating capacity lies there. Icebreakers and northern agriculture are other cold-climate concerns that properly could be Canadian prerogatives, as is learning how to keep our construction industry productive when the snow starts to fall.

In addition to climate, Canada's geography creates specific Canadian needs. We have the longest coastline and the largest continental shelf in the world. In 1.4 million square miles (or 40% of Canada's land area) lie half of our ultimate potential in oil reserves. No one has dealt with the magnitude of the problems that exist here. Off the coast of Newfoundland, for example, there is the hazard of drifting icebergs so massive they scrape the ocean floor; there are vast annual drifts of Arctic pack ice; and there are seasonal sea storms as severe as any found on the oceans.

Because one quarter of the world's fresh water lies within our boundaries we have a special interest in both using it (fish-farming, transportation, tourism) and in keeping it usable (free of pollution, accessible).

Due to the immense distances we need to span in transportation and communications we have impressive records in associated technologies. An expanded expertise in microcomputers is vital here, as is the development of communication satellites. Canada a century ago recognized the urgency of a trans-continental train in maintaining national unity. Today, with separatist movements in Quebec, the Maritimes, the West and among Indians, our unity is under no smaller strain, and modern transportation and communication facilities no less urgent.

While Canada's research and development activities could be expanded, we will never produce much more than a small share of the world's knowledge. This makes it especially advantageous for us to direct our research to produce to advantage, to produce for the goals of our evolving economy. Recycling technologies, renewable energy technologies, and advanced technologies to make products more efficient and more useful are all attainable.

But without a conscious decision by Canadians to improve our designs these goals may not be first realized here. Old ideas, such as those behind planned obsolescence, are still strongly entrenched, and they die hard.

11 *Planned Obsolescence as an Obsolete Idea*

WHAT DO YOU do if you manufacture something practically every family already owns? Wait until it breaks down before you sell a replacement? Convince the family it really needs two of them? Dream up a new and improved product?

If you're Kodak, and your profits depend on the sales of new cameras, this is what you do, and why you do it:

> On the one hand, the longer a particular generation of cameras can be sold, the more profitable it will become. On the other hand, amateur photographers tend to use less film as their cameras age and lose their novelty; hence it is critical that Kodak keep the camera population eternally young by bringing on new generations from time to time. In each successive generation, Kodak tries to . . . encourage even greater film consumption per camera—a higher "burn rate" as the company calls it. In general, the idea is to introduce as few major new models as possible while bringing in frequent minor changes powerful enough to stimulate new purchases. Kodak has become a master of this marketing strategy. (*Fortune*, September, 1976)

Kodak is proud of its marketing technique. It has worked with great success making Kodak one of the world's foremost organizations. It employs tens of thousands of employees at generous salaries and is widely considered a model corporate citizen. It is companies like Kodak that make our economy what it is today.

In the words of a leading industrial designer, "our whole economy is based on planned obsolescence, and everybody who can read without moving his lips should know it by now. We make good products, we induce people to buy them, and then next year we deliberately introduce something that will make those products old fashioned, out of date, obsolete.... It isn't organized waste. It's a sound contribution to the economy."

The logic behind planned obsolescence is so simple a child can understand it. The sooner things become obsolete, the sooner they'll need to be replaced. This creates more employment for the labour force and more profits for the manufacturer. The employment gives people the money to buy more and more goods, while the profits let the manufacturer produce more and more. Everybody ends up ahead.

Not only children understand this.

In 1977, federal Finance Minister Jean Chrétien exhorted Canadians to spend their money (on what was not important) to stimulate the economy and help pull the country out of its recession. He later modified his position, still encouraging Canadians to spend their money but for Canadian products. This echoed President Eisenhower's solution to America's recession a quarter of a century earlier. When asked at a press conference, what to do, his one-word reply was:

"Buy."

"Buy what?" he was asked.

"Anything."

President Eisenhower also modified his position, later saying the public should buy only what it needs and wants.

The concept of planned obsolescence predates President Eisenhower. It was a notion actively promoted through leading trade journals and the business press decades earlier. Its originator, a salesman by the name of J. George Frederick, called it "progressive obsolescence." His idea was to indoctrinate the well-heeled with the habit of "buying more goods on the basis of obsolescence in efficiency, economy, style or taste." This was the late 1920s.

By the mid-thirties, the term was being called "outmoded durability" and supported by nine out of ten business experts surveyed for an article subtitled, "If Merchandise Does Not Wear Out Faster, Factories Will be Idle, People Unemployed." These experts preferred to sell, at $1, a chair lasting one year to a chair selling at $1.25 but lasting five years.

Engineering associations became interested in the idea as well. They enlisted speakers to talk of "the desirability of building automobiles with a limited life." When discussing trucks, the emphasis was put on designing their parts for "controllable wear." During the Second World War this view was shelved, but only temporarily. It came back with a vengeance during the 1950s. Planned obsolescence was an idea whose time had come.

Again, it was the business press that promoted the plan. One article advocated " ... the need for a broad policy of planned obsolescence in order to take the maximum advantage of our potential for productivity and technological progress." It appealed "to those men who are responsible for the design engineering of these products. First of all, it means that design for planned obsolescence becomes a legitimate objective." Another, entitled: "Planned Obsolescence: Prescription for Tired Markets?" stressed that "it is clear that a pattern of successful style obsolescence must eventually be reinforced by a decrease in the durability of the product."

An editorial, entitled "Product Death Rates—A Desirable Concept?" reported that "it is of marked interest to learn from a highly-placed engineer in a prominent portable radio manufacturing company that his product is designed to last *not* more than three years." The editorial, in a burst of idealistic fervour, predicted that "planned existence spans of products may well become one of the greatest boosts to the economy since the origination of time payments. Such a philosophy demands a new look at engineering ethics. Respected engineers have long sought to build the best, or the lightest, or the fastest or at the lowest cost—but few have been called upon to provide all of this with a predetermined life-span."

Support for planned obsolescence was not absolute in all quarters. The Society of Industrial Designers was lectured by a noted Harvard professor that "you have been called upon to put a varnish of appearance and attractiveness on things that are going down badly.... You are increasing the cost of things and their service. I call this cheapening design, and you will eventually lose your reputation." But this was considered no more than an effete view from academic circles. Hard-headed business logic dictated otherwise.

There are three ways a product can become obsolete. Its function can become outmoded, such as the horse and buggy or the vacuum-tube radio. Its style can become passé, such as the mini-skirt or the double-tracked razor blade. Or it can be made to break down or wear out, such as almost everything else.

Planning the obsolescence of a product is not always difficult. To establish its probable lifetime you often have only to determine the lifespan of its weakest link. Plastics, for example, that look fine in the showroom but crack or discolour in home use work admirably although they often cost more than durable plastics that could last as long as the product. Using a plastic part inside an appliance where metal is required lets it snap or warp, conveniently leading to a fast failure rate. Reducing the gauge on metals, the size and number of bolts, and the quality of interior finishes where rust protection is important will also do the job while saving in material costs.

Planning obsolescence can often require extensive research, testing, and time. But if the company succeeds well enough in making its products useless, it can more than recover those costs. The danger lies in miscalculating the delicate balance between the length of a product's life and the length of its warranty. In the early days of planned obsolescence, before this relationship could be fine-tuned, it created a great deal of embarrassment for manufacturers. Hotpoint distributors, for example, were plagued with six to seven repair calls a year for their 1955, '56, and '57 models. This was considerably higher than the failure rate for the appliance industry as a whole—two to three breakdowns a year for each appliance sold. Industry's reaction was to reduce the warranty period, in some cases to several weeks.

Meanwhile, rugs which used to last 10 to 15 years were developed to wear out in less than two; furniture makers learned to select knotty wood to make the frames of sofas break under reasonable strain. For outdoor furniture, used only seasonally, webbing was selected which would give way when someone weighing more than 140 pounds sat on it. Although this may have been fine for the economy, it became a nuisance for people tired of returning to the store to make the same purchase over and over again.

The trade journals, which used to report proudly that "many housewares manufacturers are cheapening the quality of their products, and are likely to step up this process even more in the months to come," began to sense a consumer backlash. One editor pointed out that "the doctrine of planned obsolescence is carried out so far that the product can scarcely hold together for shipment. And maintenance is so difficult and unreliable that replacement is easier." Another warned that current practices must stop. "The customer will accept the planned obsolescence of products, but he will not accept being made into a messenger boy, carrying merchandise to and from the repair shop."

Some manufacturers were able to develop programs of planned obsolescence with more grace than others, General Electric chief among them. Had GE not been brought to court by the U.S. government on an unrelated matter, its internal memoranda might never have come to light. One memo introduced as evidence detailed a company engineer's progress in shortening the life of flashlights. Originally, the flashlight's bulbs outlasted three batteries. Research had developed a bulb which would break down after two batteries. The engineer proposed to his superior further work to bring down the bulb life to one battery. "If this is done," the memo pointed out, "we estimate it would result in increasing our flashlight business approximately 60%." Another piece of evidence from the

GE suit advised one of the company's licencees of the following approved change: "The design life of the 2330 Lamp has been changed from 300 back to 200 hours.... It is understood that no publicity or other announcement will be made of the change."

The light bulb industry continues to be a leader in planned obsolescence. Japanese manufacturers are able to offer Canadian distributors two lines of bulbs at the same price, one lasting twice as long as the other. Because of the replacement market, the Canadian wholesalers prudently pick the bulbs that burn out better.

But building a badder mousetrap has its limits. The business press related the new consensus: "If we are to create obsolescence ... and find ourselves making products that don't last too long, we must rely on something besides mechanical deficiencies to create a replacement market." That something is style. And when industry unified behind the idea of promoting regular style changes to make existing products obsolete, it did so with enthusiasm.

Westinghouse explained that a complete redesign of products each year was too costly. "But changes only in decorative trim will satisfy the dealer, please the customer and effectively obsolete the previous year's model." Frigidaire, the now defunct refrigerator company, decided to go right to the public with its sales campaign slogan: Planned Product Obsolescence. The head of Frigidaire proudly proclaimed "we have committed ourselves to a program of planned product obsolescence." A trade journal article entitled "Planned Obsolescence Creates Sharp Rift in Appliance Industry" reported frictions in the growing trend. The rift was caused by some thinking that industry wasn't doing enough to create obsolescence.

The gospel of obsolescence spread beyond its traditional domain. A home builder shook his fist at several hundred other developers at a convention and told them to get out there and create more obsolescence. A plywood association spread the slogan "Every family needs two homes." And a national business magazine reported that "the home building industry is finally taking a cue from the automobile industry ... like the automakers the home builders are trying to foster 'planned obsolescence by putting more emphasis on styling, etc.'" People who couldn't afford an all-new home were urged to at least spruce up by buying new fixtures for their "used homes."

Another business publication urged that "it is not only our privilege to obsolete the minimum home and many home furnishings, it is our obligation. We are obligated to work on obsolescence as our contribution to a healthy growing society." The 54-inch standard double bed was replaced by twin beds, queen-sized and king-sized beds. Televisions went for the slim look. Refrigerators—all seven major brands—made the switch from round corners to square corners in the same year. With the same display of teamwork, each year saw a different colour for appliances come into vogue. The kitchen had become as self-conscious as its well-dressed occupants.

If the home furnishings industry took its cue from the automobile industry, the automobile industry had taken its cue from the fashion industry—the most experienced obsoleters of them all. Through collusion, fashion designers decide what's acceptable for the coming season. New styles are carefully tailored to avoid any possibility of fashionable use of last season's styles.

The industry has become sophisticated. Once it naïvely thought merely raising or lowering the hemline of a dress would effectively obsolete it. To its dismay, it learned that budget-conscious women were raising hems and then lowering them with each dictate of the designer. The designers were not to be so easily undone. They quickly put an end to this habit by changing the shape of the shoulders or adjusting the waist as well as the hemline. For a female to be fashionable she must pay.

But while the fashion industry had the most historic success it also had the most dismal failure. Unlike females, the male of the species could not be so regularly refashioned. Millions of dollars were spent redressing this anomaly. Obsolescence was pushed as the major marketing trend in men's wear.

The leather industry began a campaign to persuade women to buy distinctive accessories for their husbands. The shoe industry responded by saying "we will be making shoes for men, women, and youngsters so distinctive that anyone who clings to the old styles will be conspicuous." The flare of coats began to fluctuate. Men began being advised that their shirt collars were out of date. The tie swelled out and the shirt tapered in. Eyeglass frames became eyesores when their look changed in shape or material. Suddenly men needed coiffures as much as women. Purses for gentlemen became quite proper, and promotion of male cosmetics stopped drawing snickers.

The industry that brought women the spiked heel (giving them the focussed impact of an elephant for a given spot hit by the heel) brought the male the elevator shoe.

Fashion taught the modern male how to walk tall.

No company learned more from the fashion industry than General Motors, the first technological company to tinker with styling. Supporting the concept of "artificial obsolescence," one of GM's foremost chairmen said "if it had not been for the annual model change, the automobile as we know it today would not be produced in volume and would be priced so that relatively few could afford to own one. Our customers would have no incentive or reason to buy a new car until their old one wore out."

General Motors instituted its policy in response to Ford's disconcerting habit of producing the same Model T in volume and pricing it so that great numbers could afford to own one. Over fifteen years, Ford lowered its price from $780 to $290 by sticking to one basic design, with only technological improvements being made. Since GM couldn't match Ford in either production know-how or pricing, it competed on the basis of style. It competed so successfully that Ford almost went bankrupt before grudgingly agreeing to get into a new production line each year. By 1940 cars were kept just five-and-a-half years. By 1960 the time to trade-in shortened to two-and-a-quarter years.

The annual model changes meant a deterioration in the quality of the car. It often takes years to get the bugs out, even if the producer cares to. In the pre-1960s sentiment for planned obsolescence, the producer openly did not care to. Officials of an industrial-design firm asserted that "alloys are designed to rust instead of last. There seems to be no doubt that bodies of present-day cars could be made to last much longer than they now do, but manufacturers are fully aware that if they make their cars too durable future sales will suffer; consumers will naturally tend to keep their cars longer before turning them in if bodies have well resisted corrosion and other types of damage that mar their appearance."

Tires were made to wear out faster. One fleet of 430 cars found tire life down 25% to 15,000 miles.

Automobile mufflers in 1958 had half the life expectancy of mufflers installed in 1948. A major steel company tried to sell the automobile manufacturers a lead-coated steel it developed which would guarantee the muffler would last the life of the car. They refused, probably not because of price. A life-time muffler would have increased the price by eight cents.

Although car registration rose by only one million in North America from 1957 to 1958, the number of car breakdowns leapt up by six million. In a moment of guilt, a Chrysler vice president admitted in a *Time* interview that auto service was bad and the quality of cars not as good as ten years earlier. "The auto industry," he affirmed, "has treated the public badly, to say it mildly."

The twenties and thirties saw major technological innovations in the automotive industry: advances such as shock absorbers, the balloon tire and four-wheel brakes were introduced almost every year. This was before the era of intense style changes, when the undue emphasis on styling shifted funds away from engineering to appearance. These innovations produced obsolescence as well, but an obsolescence based on superior products and lower cost. Progress can be readily appreciated when it takes the form of jet travel replacing the prop plane or the transistor putting the tube to rest. This can easily be seen as an advance for society. It is more difficult to appreciate when, after succeeding in making a certain styling esthetically appealing, after succeeding in having it adopted and accepted, progress takes the form of expending great effort producing and selling an arbitrarily changed design. It is more difficult to accept the idea that building something to break down somehow helps our economy to grow.

If things are made to last half as long, it is the equivalent of charging twice as much for them. This can only make the goods less accessible to people, and more likely to impoverish the less fortunate ones. The deprivation that results is hardly a boon to the economy. People are forced to divert a greater percentage of their money to necessary purchases.

Having workers produce twice as many things that last half as long is the equivalent of having them produce goods with a normal life span and paying them to sit idle half the time—hardly productive. Making things last half as long also uses twice the amount of materials. This is the equivalent of disposing of half our valuable natural resources without compensation—not a sound business practice.

All the work resulting from planned obsolescence is unproductive work, and all the extra goods that stem from it are tantamount to garbage. They are merely dumped, with nothing to show for the work. An economy dedicated to waste on a massive scale tends to suffer.

The American involvement in Vietnam was thought a great boon to its economy. The United States had full employment during the war, with industry working at close to full capacity. But industry's product was not used productively. The American economy spent $30 billion per year on Vietnam and got nothing back for it. It might as well have thrown the $30 billion into the Vietnamese jungle. The United States has never quite recovered from that extravagence. It went into a recession after the war; its dollar has steadily devalued against the currencies of its Western European allies, and it no longer commands the same position of dominance in the Western economy.

Assume we didn't have planned obsolescence and everything lasted twice as long, that our goods didn't go out of fashion every year and they didn't wear out as often. Since we'd have to replace everything half as often, we'd be twice as well off.

Consider the individual who purchases a car. If his tolerance is similar to others, the car starts to be more trouble than it's worth after about three years. Let's say he replaces it every three years, and that (trade-ins and all considered) it costs him $5,000 each time. To run it for six years costs him $10,000. Now what if that car could give him trouble-free service for six years? After the first three years, he could use the $5,000 he would have spent for a replacement car to buy an additional car. For the same amount of money, he could own two cars. If he didn't need a second car, or if he didn't want a more modern model, he could use the extra $5,000 to finish his basement or buy a mink coat for his mother-in-law or pad his bank account or take an extended vacation.

The benefit to the individual is clear. The benefit to the overall economy is also clear. If the individual decides to buy a second car with the $5,000, the automobile company will break even. It will have sold him the same two cars. If he decides to spend the money on his basement or his mother-in-law or a trip, a furrier or a carpenter or a travel agent may benefit instead. If he puts it into the bank, the bank will lend it to someone who'll spend it for him. Either way, the economy as a whole will not be suffering. The same amount of money will be circulating, generating jobs and profits. Meanwhile, with everyone being twice as well off, people will have more money to spend. Many will rise from the ranks of poverty and not need financial support from the rest of society. The economy as a whole will function at a higher level of prosperity.

The ones to feel sorry for will be those corporations with their vision fixed firmly in place, unable to adapt to changing markets. There won't be too many of those. The Hudson's Bay Company, founded 300 years ago, went into the department store business, the distillery business, and the oil business as a hedge against the unlikely prospect that the beaver pelt business might drop off.

Diversification in business has been a long-going trend. Canadian Pacific runs restaurants; ITT bakes bread. This trend exists partially because spreading investments spreads the risk of financial decline, but also because large profitable companies often generate too much capital for all of it to be reinvested in the same business. When ITT met the public's demand for telephone service they could have decided to increase business by producing telephones that needed regular replacing, and growing from there. Instead they chose to branch out by investing in equally lucrative ventures elsewhere. The public didn't lose out on its telephones and the company didn't lose out on its profits.

Industry itself will benefit in other ways. A factory doesn't only make things; it also consumes a great deal in plant equipment and materials. Eliminating planned obsolescence of industrial goods will improve industry's profitability. Improved profitability and more durable products will allow it to be more competitive, giving it a greater share of foreign markets.

But unlike the benefit to the consumer, the benefit to industry would not be immediate. Several years would pass before the first effects would be felt, and several years more before the overall benefit to the economy would filter through to individual companies. During this period of sure gains, companies would be uncertain of their particular gains. It would be a time of change when the relative standings of companies could be rearranged.

And then some companies might become obsolete themselves.

While eliminating planned obsolescence may seem desirable to industry, it has never seemed urgent. Businesses that do well don't protest that they're not doing better. Businesses that go bankrupt are in no position to protest.

And with nothing being ventured, nothing's being changed.

12 *The New Obsolescence*

PLANNED OBSOLESCENCE WAS at its height in 1960, when appliances needed twice the number of repairs they needed before the Second World War; when Sylvania's director of research predicted that within three years servicing a TV set would cost two and a half times what the original set itself cost; when an automatic washer or dishwasher needed two service calls to get through its first year of operation and an electric dryer or refrigerator was considered reliable because it only averaged one breakdown in its first year of service. By 1960, products were being designed to be practically irreparable. Toasters were riveted so that a repairman had to spend nearly an hour just getting to the working parts. To replace a 15-cent light-bulb or 10-cent spring complex appliances had to be dismantled. This tended to discourage repairs, as did the practice of not stocking parts. Two-thousand-dollar pumps couldn't be repaired because two-dollar parts would be unavailable.

Despite these efforts, enough products broke down belonging to enough people wanting them fixed to make the repair business big business. The muffler-replacement market alone was worth a half-billion dollars. Since it could never have existed had the automakers originally installed mufflers that lasted the life of the car, they rightfully took credit for the emergence of this new industry. Yet the automakers weren't benefitting. This struck all manufacturers as a great injustice.

Manufacturers responded by becoming affiliated with the repair industry to share in its profits. Never again would they have to fret that others would benefit from their broken merchandise at their expense. Whether the customer repaired it or junked it, producing an inferior product would pay. The manufacturers' enthusiasm for planned obsolescence was now unqualified.

The consumer didn't share in this enthusiasm. To the producer's disappointment, consumer complaints showed no appreciation for the benefits of planned obsolescence. Product breakdowns drove many to the point of exasperation. Despite industry efforts to educate the consumer, planned obsolescence became dirty words. The long-feared consumer backlash began.

Industry decided the public would never understand; it would never change. Instead industry itself would have to change. No more would industry continue to promote in an above-board manner something the public found unpalatable. Instead it decided to promote it privately.

Planned obsolescence, once a household term, disappeared from business and trade publications almost overnight. Industry spokesmen adopted a very different vocabulary. Common euphemisms such as "product death rates" and "time to failure," were replaced by the more positive sounding "product life cycle." The sorest source of dissatisfaction with planned obsolescence—frequent product breakdowns—was decisively dealt with, despite great regrets and reservations. No amount of public relations could rescue it; industry knew that if it were to save the patient's life, amputating this limb was unavoidable. Product breakdowns would have to go.

The rate at which televisions broke down decreased by 50% in eight years. The more reliable refrigerator was also made to break down less often, although it took fourteen years for its rate to drop 50%. Overall, service costs for appliances declined dramatically. In the 1955-73 period, while the consumer price index rose 66% and the cost of household repair services rose 106%, the service costs for appliances, radios and televisions dropped by 17%. This was a remarkable performance for industry, the more so since it was able to make products break down less often without increasing their real life. In fact, if there was any trend at all over this period, it was toward a further shortening of the life of products.

Industry managed—in one of its greatest coups—to increase the reliability of its products without having to compromise on their obsolescence. It was able to maintain the significant gains made over previous decades, while defusing planned obsolescence as a public issue.

From a technical point of view, there is no question that longer-lasting products can be made. This is freely agreed to by manufacturers. Each component in a product could be designed for maximum durability. Materials could be selected for wear and corrosion resistance. Gear trains could replace rubber belts and pulleys. Sensitive parts could be sealed from the atmosphere. Circuits could be made more tolerant of variations in humidity, altitude, line voltage, and human error. There are no great expenses here.

Or products could be built so that everything is easily and cheaply repairable. Even cosmetic items such as exterior panels, doors and trim could be renewable or replaceable so that appearance would be maintained as readily as operating effectiveness. The costs of replacement parts or service labour could be reduced considerably by greater use of modular components and more standardization of parts.

Ironically, the improvement of products is generally accompanied by a reduction in price. This makes the statement from a director of product engineering at Whirlpool that "If we would look closely at our products, it would be apparent that improvements can be made at little or no expense" an understatement. Historically, prices have dropped when products have improved.

Improvements have often come about by more appropriate, more efficient use of materials. A 1% reduction in materials cost can have the same effect on profit as a 20% increase in sales. The world's first electronic digital computer weighed 30 tons and ran on 18,000 vacuum tubes. Over the course of 30 years, it has become somewhat more streamlined. The modern micro-computer can outperform its ancestor, is able to make its calculations twenty times faster on an area a fraction of an inch square weighing less than an ounce. It has come down in price by more than 99.9% — better than the best discount retailers offer. Almost as good a bargain is the transistor. Between 1960 and 1970 its price dropped 99%.

The calculator is an example of a consumer product which has decreased in size and cost while improving in quality. So is the television set, the telephone, the transistor radio, the copying machine, the camera, and the hearing aid. Over the last 50 years, 100 years, 150 years, or 200 years, the true prices of products (taking inflation into account) have been dropping for virtually every commodity. About the only exception, over the last two centuries, has been the shoe. The inability to reduce the price of footwear ranks as one of mankind's more curious failings.

It is overemphasis on style that holds back technological innovation. If you took a can opener to your late-model refrigerator or washing machine, and compared what lies beneath its exterior trim to the interior of a 20- or 25-year-old model, you'd see little difference. The gear transmission, compressor systems, and other mechanisms have remained essentially unchanged.

Companies will often hold back technological improvements from the market until sales of existing models decline. The stereo patent was taken out in 1931 by an Englishman, and several American companies soon acquired the rights. But they didn't market stereos because hi-fis were selling well. It wasn't until the late 1950s, when many families already owned new hi-fis and demand for new phonographs was dropping off that they decided to introduce the stereo and outmode the hi-fi. In the parlance of the fifties, this was planned obsolescence. Today, the same decision would be based on the "product life cycle." The product-life-cycle concept began when an accountant noticed that products have a great deal in common with human beings. They both are born, go through various stages, and then, sooner or later, die.

Psychologists have done a considerable amount of research

into the human stages. Marketing analysts took over the task in studying product life. The first phase is the introduction phase. This is similar to a baby being born. Announcements are made and there's often a lot of fanfare. The second phase is the development phase. The full value of the product is not yet appreciated, and its potential remains high. This is a learning stage, with production techniques often changing. Next comes the growth phase. More and more people are able to appreciate the product. Production techniques are standardized and tend to larger-scale and longer runs. Then the product becomes mature. Production runs reach the limit of plant capacity and economies of plant scale are common. The product has to face more and more competition. As the demand for the product starts to drop, it enters its decline. Different advertising methods and sales approaches are needed to keep it alive. But it's on its deathbed. It's only a matter of time before it enters its last phase—death.

The idea is to predict the death stage. Then—in a sort of industrial euthanasia—the product can be put out of its misery. Needless funds won't be foolishly spent propping up a product whose days are numbered. Those funds can instead be shifted out of its advertising and promotion budget and into the research and development budget of a new product. Most predictions of a product's impending demise prove to be true. The marketer's ability to predict when a product dies is somewhat similar to the ability Billy the Kid had to predict human deaths. His finger is on the trigger.

When a product's sales slip, and it's thought to be approaching the death stage, its advertising budget gets shot down and the product is left to its own devices. Not surprisingly, stripped of this support, its sales will suffer even more. Panic ensues in corporate boardrooms, new products are hastily launched, and the old product is left to founder. When it finally dies, company executives knowingly pat themselves on the back, pleased at the accuracy of their prediction.

Occasionally, products are rescued which were given up for dead. Ipana toothpaste was marketed until 1968, when it was abandoned in favour of new brands. In early 1969, two Minnesota businessmen picked up the Ipana name, left the package unchanged, and with hardly any promotion managed $250,000 in sales in the first seven months of operation. Five years later, it was still used by more than one and a half million adults. Considering the limited resources of the owners, it would have been in an even stronger position had Ipana remained under its original ownership.

Du Pont decided to ignore the product life cycle concept in the 1940s, and 1950s, despite the lack of professionalism this showed. Nylon, originally used primarily for military purposes in rope and parachutes, might not be around today had the company believed that nylon's declining sales curve signalled death. Instead Du Pont entered the consumer textile market. Women switched from silk to nylon stockings, children and teenagers began wearing hosiery as well, and an almost-dead product was suddenly very much alive. Had Du Pont stopped there, nylon consumption would have levelled off at 50 million pounds annually by 1962. Instead it introduced the durable stretch sock, put nylon in rugs, tires, bearings, and other products, and brought its consumption to 500 million pounds by 1962.

The idea that products have lifespans similar to humans is hard for many to support. Listerine has succeeded in keeping the lion's share of its market for decades despite strongly supported new brands. Seven-Up, once thought a touch-and-go proposition because of its image as a mixer, found new life as the "Uncola." Products such as Jell-O, Maxwell House Coffee, Planter's Peanuts, Tide detergent and Colgate toothpaste have all been long-lived yet are still full of vitality.

Harder still to support is confidence in the ability to predict when a product will die naturally. A study found that business was able to predict the date of a product's death no more accurately than a computer picking dates at random. Yet the concept of product life spans remains conventional wisdom. Instead of emphasizing the prolonging of the productive life of existing products, business puts the emphasis on new products. The odds are four to one against a new product being a winner, but like a new baby in the family, the new product gets all the attention while older brands are neglected. Meanwhile, companies that have invested millions to build goodwill for a particular brand walk away from it and spend more millions on a new brand that differs only in that it has no consumer confidence.

Product life cycles try to predict the length of time a product, or its brand name, can be marketed. They do not try to predict the functional life of a particular product. But how long a product can give dependable service is an indispensable piece of information. Until recently, this judgment has been made by educated guesses. The guessers have often been profound illiterates.

The U.S. Defense Department was the first organization to systematically analyze the many costs involved in the purchase of a product. Among the factors it recognized were the product price, equipment life, installation, manpower, the labour rate, the mean time between failures, the mean time to repair, costs of a preventative maintenance cycle, the maintenance labour rate, the costs of parts and supplies as a percent of product price, input power and the cost per kilowatt.

Leaving out one or more factors can destroy the accuracy of the prediction, as industry has discovered to its regret. One company's loss from a single unit of processing equipment used to fabricate a steel product totalled over $420,000 annually. The company was only aware of $150,000 of it—the balance was overlooked because one factor wasn't considered.

A company purchasing trucks asked the manufacturer to analyze the total costs involved in using disc brakes as opposed to shoe brakes. The disc brakes were lighter, cost less, and were included as standard equipment by the truckmaker to keep his trucks competitive. But disc brakes broke down more often. The additional cost of having disc brakes, including the lost profit due to additional downtime, came to $143,785 per truck over its six-year life. It was a sum the purchaser would never have guessed.

A company owning a fleet of cars and trucks analyzed its costs over the life of the machines. It found that cars with a $3,600 sticker price had total costs of $9,200 while cars costing

$3,950 cost $8,300 overall. Trucks costing the identical amount when first purchased differed by over $3,000 after operating costs were considered.

The total cost of a product—its life-cycle cost—can be several times its initial cost. A colour TV, gas range, or vacuum cleaner will generally have an average life-cycle cost of about twice the initial purchase price. That means you can expect a $700 colour TV set to cost an extra $700 in installation costs, repairs, and electricity over its useful life. Its total cost to you will be $1400.

A dishwasher, black-and-white TV, or electric typewriter's life-cycle cost will be two-and-a-half times the purchase price. For an air conditioner, electric dryer, frost-free refrigerator, or washing machine expect to pay three-and-a-half times the initial price over its lifespan. An electric range's total cost can be four-and-a-half times its purchase price, and a freezer can cost five times the original price.

These figures are all averages. Choosing a particular brand of electric dryer or typewriter or television set can lead to large savings. The U.S. government, for example, was offered two apparently comparable air conditioners, one for $300 each, the other for $301.19 each. An analysis of their life-cycle costs showed the cheaper model to cost $132 more than its competitor. The government invested the extra $1.19 per machine and saved several million dollars in the process.

This kind of information, which is increasingly being made available to government and industry, should be available to the consumer. There is little point in letting consumers know the initial price of a product when it bears no relationship to what they're letting themselves in for. Along with the purchase price, consumers should be given the life-cycle cost of the product. This cost can be presented as the average cost, per year, of buying and keeping a product in good repair over its lifespan.

One television set, for example, might cost $600 to purchase and $900 to operate over its estimated 10-year life. Another might cost $700 to purchase and $500 to operate over a 12-year lifespan. The first set's life-cycle cost is $1,500. Over 10 years, its total cost to the purchaser equals $150 per year. The second set, costing $1,200 over twelve years, only costs $100 per year to own. Without being made aware of their life-cycle costs, the price-conscious consumer might well buy the set for $600. He still may, if he prefers its style, or its picture. But if he finds the products comparable, and wants to base his purchase on price, the price tags he should be comparing should say "$150 per year" and "$100 per year"; not "$600" and "$700." Since most people buy on credit, a lower initial purchase price need never be the determining factor when purchasing a product.

The lifespan of a product is not necessarily the time until the first thing goes wrong with it, or the longest period in which it can be kept going. A car need not be scrapped when the windshield wiper won't stop, or kept on the road until it's no longer recognizable as a vehicle. But when a consumer purchases a car, he should be entitled to know how long it can be kept working and looking reasonably the same. If a manufacturer wants to advertise a car lasting ten years, then more than the motor should last that long. The life-cycle costs of the car will reflect how much the purchaser can expect to pay to replace the tires when they wear out, how much rust-proofing protection will cost, the expected fuel consumption, and every other pertinent factor. It can even include the interest payments if he's buying the car on time.

It's only fair.

Once everything is priced on this basis, a revolution will take place in the manufacturing industry. Right now, the manufacturer benefits when he can keep his costs down. Once life-cycle pricing is adopted, the manufacturer will benefit when he can keep his customers' costs down. It's a small change in orientation but its ramifications are sweeping.

Life-cycle pricing will do more than put the emphasis on the quality and durability of goods. Many goods won't last in Canada if they aren't made for the Canadian climate. Life-cycle pricing will put the emphasis on what the needs of Canadians are. It will favour those products designed specifically for Canadians, or people whose needs are very similar to Canadians.

An American boat manufacturer, producing a fine vessel for

California waters, may suddenly see his price advantage over Canadian manufacturers disappear. If the boat was designed for southern climes, its durability will drop and its life-cycle price will rise for our colder climate. A Canadian manufacturer, conscious that winter warps the hull and makes the motor fussy, will have more of the market for himself.

Life-cycle pricing will set *de facto* Canadian standards. The government won't have to step in and raise trading barriers to protect Canadian manufacturing. With the Canadian market defining itself in terms of the life cycles of products used in Canada, whoever produces with the Canadian market in mind can't help but benefit.

Few Canadian manufacturers produce with the Canadian market in mind. Because of massive competition from foreign manufacturers and the lack of Canadian standards, their objectives have become blurred. Canadian firms have often become Americanized. Life-cycle pricing will repatriate them.

Foreign-owned manufacturers in Canada don't generally produce products designed especially for Canadians. They more often reproduce foreign products for the Canadian market. When these products are suitable, they will compete favourably with the life-cycle price of Canadian products. But when they're not, as will become increasingly the case, they'll be faced with the choice of either accepting lower sales, leaving the market entirely or competing in the Canadian market as a Canadian business. If they leave the market or accept lower sales, Canadian companies will pick up the slack.

When American companies start to compete on our terms, the products they develop will not necessarily be suited for manufacture in their home market. The bulk of their sales will be in Canada, and countries with needs like Canada's, such as the Scandinavian countries and the USSR. They will choose to manufacture in Canada, keep their technology in Canada, and export from Canada whenever possible.

But whether the products are manufactured by Canadian-owned firms or foreign-owned firms, the research and development behind them will stay here. Canada's investment in technology will begin paying off, secure in the knowledge Canadian discoveries will be developed here. This expertise will form the basis of our future trade. With the world's store of cold-weather technology centred here, any country that experiences cold weather will be a potential client for our products. Our knowledge will find widespread applications.

The potential market extends far beyond those countries that are predominantly cold. Most of Europe has areas that become cold in winter. But a country such as Spain—with most of its concerns concentrated on problems associated with heat—could not justify developing industries for the needs of its cold plateaux.

Many of our products don't need to be designed for the cold. Most household appliances, for example, will have the same durability in El Paso, Texas, as they will in Moose Jaw or Moosonee. Here Canadian products will have superior life-cycle costs when their operating costs are lower and they last longer.

An American producer of television sets may not find it in his interest to cater to the Canadian market by making a set that consumes less electricity or lasts longer. The Canadian producer who is willing to develop a TV that does can be fairly confident there will be a market for it. The historic advantage in marketing and mass producing that the Americans have enjoyed will evaporate when their products are marketed on the basis of life-cycle pricing.

Because we still don't have this kind of pricing, the real costs of obsolescence are easy to ignore. The concept of planned obsolescence has never really been challenged—when faced with public protest it merely went underground. Despite current trends toward more durable goods, occasional evidence here or there of our society abandoning short-life goods ignores the momentum of the trend toward planned obsolescence. The economic recession of the 1970s slowed the progress of planned obsolescence much as the economic needs of the Second World War did a generation earlier.

But all the while, planned obsolescence has been making quiet inroads. Our buildings are now designed to last thirty years and eminent architects are suggesting our skyscrapers be designed with easy demolition in mind. Throughout history, the value of architecture has transcended narrow goals. Buildings have been the most visible legacy of the past. Each society's, each era's aspirations have translated themselves into distinctive and enduring physical forms. Investments made centuries earlier are still enriching our lives today. Yet we are considering discounting the value of these assets in the future. Assets into which we will be pouring immense amounts of our productive ability are to be made as obsolete and as disposable as automobiles.

Continued acceptance of planned obsolescence has clouded our judgment as to what is efficient and what is not. It has obscured our purpose in doing things to the point that the purpose has become to undo them.

Cars on the road in the 1930s can still be seen, functioning as well as ever. Their owners derive great pleasure from them. The prospects of the 1980 car giving similar pleasure to the automobile aficionado of the year 2020, despite what some see as technological improvements, are not favourable.

Furniture hundreds of years old has appreciated in value and maintained its utility. Measured on an efficiency scale, it has proven to be a remarkably wise investment. Yet despite this lesson, similar efficiencies are not reached for today.

A full accounting of planned obsolescence involves more than life-cycle costing. It requires a closer look at the human and physical capital that is squandered with such extravagance. It also requires a closer look at the motive force that has kept this machine respectable even as our economy has been faltering more and more. That motor is advertising. To put our economy in smooth running order it will need an overhaul.

13 *The Unselling of Advertising*

I

TAKE A ROCK, put it in a pretty package, give it a catchy name (the Pet Rock) and you've created an important new industry. Don't be concerned that the rock doesn't do anything—you can make that a selling feature (Pet Rocks don't need to be walked, fed or defleaded). Don't be worried about the consumer finding a better specimen in his back yard. Short of running geological tests, he can't know that. Don't concern yourself thinking he can't be persuaded to purchase rocks at all. You may have to go into the hole for awhile (it took the Pet Rock's promoter, an advertising executive, over $200,000 to make the Pet Rock concept spontaneously accepted), but given enough flattering profiles of rocks and a well-written trainer's manual, marketing problems become minor.

Most of all, don't be fooled into thinking you're conning the consumer into buying something he doesn't need. There's little personal tragedy in buying a Pet Rock. It only costs five dollars, gives a good laugh, and is easily disposed of. If people want to spend their money on Pet Rocks, or anything else that gives them pleasure, why shouldn't they? If lighting their cigars with five dollar bills is what makes them happy, who has the right to tell them to do otherwise?

Our right to buy what we want when we want is not at issue. It's unlikely any government will pass laws forbidding rash purchases, and if it does (as with laws forbidding other forms of imprudence such as suicide) it's unlikely they'll lend themselves to enforcement. The issue here is not whether we should forbid dubious personal conduct; it is whether we should be encouraging it.

There's a difference between standing in a crowded room, burning dollar bills for the crowd's reaction, and standing in a crowded room, being exhorted to burn your dollar bills by the crowd. In one situation you might be made uncomfortable if you do; in the other, you might be made uncomfortable if you don't. A common response to a seemingly senseless action is some degree of repulsion, depending on how harmless the act. Someone's nausea at coarse conduct does not generally reinforce a repeat performance. But when that same conduct receives peer approval—and the act no longer seems senseless—it can be performed quite happily and quite mindlessly without sense of censure.

Advertising provides the preconditioning necessary for many senseless acts. Without it, the notion of spending five dollars for a Pet Rock would not have been acceptable. (Imagine yourself buying a pet piece of broken glass, for example.) Without advertising, burning up five dollar bills is not acceptable. With the right advertising campaign, it is wholly possible. (Burning up money is another way of making a donation to the government. It is also an imaginative way of reducing inflation. Imagine yourself caught up in a nationwide campaign to reduce inflation this way, where it becomes fashionable to be patriotic and pyromaniac at the same time. How easy would it be for you to refuse advertising's call to be a "good" Canadian?)

Few people would normally want to burn up money, or to buy Pet Rocks, or to purchase new cars every two years. At different times they may do it, but not through some instinct inherent to human nature. Their human nature has been reshaped—perverted—to make them think they want a Pet Rock when they want a laugh, or a new car when they want the status that cars represent. But their wants are no longer their own. They've been created for them by people whose function it is to manufacture wants.

Their purpose in creating this artificial need is to get our money, money we might spend elsewhere. Their method in extracting this money is whatever works, be it reasoned explanation, distorted description, or outright misrepresentation. It is not the responsibility of the advertising industry to judge the usefulness or quality of the product it's promoting; it is its responsibility to prevent us from judging a product's usefulness or quality by focussing our attention away from its negative features and onto its positive ones.

As is often the case, when a particular item's positive features do not bear much scrutiny, we're given an unladylike cleavage to scrutinize instead.

Advertising We Don't Need

The industries which bring us the most cleavages are those with the least to bang their own breasts about. In selling liquor, for example, there's only so much to say. (Aged five years? Smooth?) Not enough to fill a page of *Playboy*. The beer and tobacco industries face similar dilemmas. Providing information, even if it's in a positive light ("our tobacco is least likely to cause cancer"), may help the consumer make a decision, but it may not help the advertiser make a dollar.

So instead of providing data they provide dreams. Instead of winning us over with irresistible arguments they try to win us over with irresistible wants.

If the beer companies could produce a study which showed that drinking beer was likely to help people meet their objectives, perhaps associating beer with a good life would have some justification. But the beer companies can't deliver the good times, only the beer. And beer has little to do with having good times or bad.

By distorting our perceptions the advertising industry prevents us from making free and rational decisions. Most people have trouble enough resisting the urge to join a bandwagon even when their inclinations tell them otherwise. Why should they also have to contend with imaginary bandwagons? There are dangers to real bandwagons as well, as any sheep newly jumped off a cliff can tell you. Letting others make your decisions for you may be reassuring for a while, but if the decisions aren't ones you can ultimately live with, the sense of security may be short-lived.

It may be comforting to know you're one of ten million Canadians who smoke (much as the passengers on the Titanic might have drawn comfort from knowing they were all in the same boat). The comfort begins to wane when you contract lung cancer. Lifestyle advertising propels existing bandwagons and builds new ones. It makes harmless and harmful products equally acceptable, basing its pitch, not on the products' qualities, but on other people's acceptance of the product. Lifestyle advertising makes us want what it tells us other people want, and when we get the thing, it uses us to convince them the product was what they really wanted all along.

Good or bad, the social urge to join bandwagons has always been with us. Whether a fad such as swallowing goldfish or a phenomenon such as Jesus Christ, the decision to jump on was an organic one, arising out of an individual social need for self-expression. But bandwagons haven't always been created for us by the same self-appointed elite for the financial benefit of third parties.

Advertisers deny that they create wants. Consumers, they say, are independent thinkers who make rational decisions based on free-market considerations. Their needs and desires originate with them. All advertising does is help satisfy those wants through increasing awareness. This is what they say, at least publicly. Privately the advertisers' attitude is less benign. The advertising process is now fundamental to almost every phase of a product's development. It would be embarrassing for a company to come out with a new toothpaste that didn't sell as planned.

Typically, the production process begins with extensive consumer testing and other market research, then proceeds from there to develop some concept of a marketing approach, including the possibilities it provides for advertising campaigns. Then estimates are made of how much advertising and promotion will be necessary to sell sufficient quantities of the toothpaste at the price desired. Only after the means of selling are settled does a company attempt to develop and produce the actual product. With the consumer's tastes tapped to see what kind of package will appeal, the company sets about to fill that package.

The new product exists not because consumers wanted another toothpaste but because the producer wanted to sell one. It succeeds not because it's a better product but because it's marketed better. It satisfies not a real need in the consumer (he didn't know he needed it until it came out), but one that arose after it was produced. The production of a new toothpaste results in the satisfaction of a want created by the production. It fills a self-created void. It exists largely for its own sake. If it didn't exist, no one would shed a tear over it.

The Effect of Advertising on Competition

Competition is the life blood of the free-enterprise system, and advertising is the lifeblood of competition. Or so the advertising industry would have us believe. An attack on advertising becomes an attack on the free-enterprise system, and then righteous indignation can be used to champion this quasi-brainwashing bulwark of democracy. The irony is that advertising helps accomplish for North America what Communist planning accomplishes for Eastern Europe—an effective stifling of competition.

Iron curtain countries curtail competition through the control of state-run monopolies. With an assured demand for its production, Communist planners can set prices at the level they desire. In Western-style economies monopolies are frowned upon, even illegal. They are universally acknowledged as being inefficient and wasteful—anathema to our democratic way of life. Instead, we curtail competition through the control of near-monopolies—the industrial giants that effectively rule our marketplace. They assure demand by predetermining it through marketing techniques. With demand assured, prices can be set at the level they desire.

Near-monopolies, called oligopolies, dominate virtually

every industrial activity in North America. There were once many automobile manufacturers; now there are four, with three dominating the market. In the United States, this kind of monopolistic control exists in cigarettes, soaps and detergents, refrigerators, computers, copper, rubber, cellulose fibers, photographic equipment, and many other areas. In each case, four or fewer firms control 60% or more of the market.

In Canada the situation is no better. In tobacco, soaps and cleaning compounds, breweries, distillers, sugar, salt, iron and steel mills, uranium, asbestos, breakfast cereals, office and store machinery, lime, petroleum refining and many other areas, four or fewer firms control 80% or more of the market. When a new product is introduced by one of these four manufacturers, a large part of its competition comes from the same manufacturer. For this and other reasons, the manufacturer usually finds it in his interest to keep the competition on gentlemanly grounds.

On either side of the border, four manufacturers (Kellogg's, General Mills, General Foods and Quaker Oats) control over 90% of the domestic production of ready-to-eat cereals. For the 20-year period ending in 1970, they introduced 150 cereal brands that differed substantially only in marketing approach.

Manufacturers generally have found it safer to compete with other producers on the basis of advertising than on the more unpredictable factors of price or product quality.

The large corporation (and the people who run it) does not try to maximize profits. Its primary goal is security, which can be assured by an adequate level of profits. Maximum profits often imply risk. If the risk succeeds, the profits accrue to the shareholders. If the risk results in a loss, the executives are held responsible. They have nothing much to gain and everything to lose.

Price cutting by one firm necessitates a similar response by the others. Too dangerous. Serious price competition invites a price collapse. Producing a genuinely better product creates the same uncertainty. There could be several rounds of improvements, destroying existing markets and newly created ones. Who knows where this would stop?

In either case, the market becomes volatile and insecure. The individual fortunes of companies (and their chief executives) will tend to fluctuate. Competition of this sort can lead to unhappy states of affairs where poor companies fail and good ones excel. Better by far to compete on the basis of "packaging," "miracle ingredients," and other imaginary differences, than on the basis of real differences. It is much easier to find a new advertising agency than a new job. Corporation executives understand this.

Original and Created Wants

There's no doubt that the wants created for us by the advertising industry become our own. Twenty years ago we may not have known how much we needed armpit deodorants, just as five years ago we didn't know how much we wanted feminine deodorant sprays. Five years from now, we may discover how much we've really wanted male deodorant sprays. The introduction of new products is cited as proof of progress; this is the fulfillment of humanity's evolution. Without advertising, how would we know what we want? How would society advance?

Advertising is necessary, but its proper function is to inform people of new products we need—not to create needs for new products. You don't need to be a seer to see what our real wants are. Canadians would be near unanimous in agreeing we need automobiles that don't rust, a cure for cancer, improved methods of public transit, Panti-Hose that won't run, and flashlight batteries that don't leak. We know such things without any education from our advertisers. What we don't know in advance is that we need striped toothpaste, cake in a can, or throwaway razors. The best that can be said about these created wants is that if we do need them, we don't need them very much. Our priorities are elsewhere.

But our priorities become perverted under the avalanche of an annual $2.5 billion advertising expenditure—well over $500 for a family of four—aimed at getting us to do what we might not otherwise want to do.

If the financial gain of the few were not allowed to dominate the desires of the many, if advertising's role were readily understood, we might demand it be accorded its proper status in society. We all take pride in our personal freedoms, including our freedom of economic choice. Once we understand that this basic human right is being curtailed, the solutions become self-evident.

14 *The Unselling of Advertising II*

ADVERTISING'S PROPER ROLE, as the industry itself will tell us, is to inform the consumer. Armed with information, he's best able to exercise his free will in selecting those products he most needs. Advertising's role should be neither to create wants nor to unduly influence the consumer. These are absolute criteria. As expressed by Tom Blakely, the president of the Association of Canadian Advertising, in a speech to the converted: "we all know that no advertisement anywhere at any time made a non-drinker start drinking or a non-smoker start smoking." Presumably he was just as confident advertising has no similar effect on use of other products.

Fine then, if advertising's role is to provide information let's help it along.

The American Marketing Association conducted a study of television advertising to see how much advertising was informative. They established fourteen types of information that an ad could provide, and then counted the "pieces" of information in each ad. The fourteen criteria were elementary: Price or Value, Packaging or Shape, Quality, Guarantees or Warranties, Performance, Safety, Components or Contents, Nutrition, Availability, Independent Research, Special Offers, Co-sponsored Research, Taste, New Ideas. Mentioning where a product could be purchased, or the size package it came in, or whether it was good value would constitute information.

The study decided that an ad containing one of these pieces of information could be considered informative. It also decided to accept all information or claims the ads made as true (and thus valid pieces of information). The results surprised even the American Marketing Association. Based on these criteria more than half of all ads had no information of any kind; about 16% of ads had two of these pieces of information; less than 1% of ads had three pieces of information.

Revelations of this sort have led to strong comments from both sides of the border. In Ontario, John Clement, former Minister of Consumer and Commercial Relations, described as "amazing... the number of broadcast commercials that contain no facts or worthwhile information." In the States, the Federal Communication Commission went further: "Those forms of advertising which are essentially non-informative in character may raise questions as to their fundamental fairness, their conformity with traditional economic justifications for advertising upon which a free and reasonably informed choice can be made, and the extent to which such advertising is designed to exploit such fears or anxieties as social acceptance or personal wellbeing without fulfilling the desire raised."

Some progress has been made in limiting lifestyle advertising. Ontario, for example, now has an outright ban on all lifestyle ads that promote beer or liquor. Lifestyle ads are those ads that lead a reader or viewer to believe that the enjoyment of a situation is enhanced or dependent upon the consumption of the product advertised.

But why stop there?

An ad campaign promoting a lifestyle is selling an ideology, not a product. As such, it more closely resembles a political campaign than an ad campaign. Support of political ideology is closely regulated by present legislation: political contributions are limited in size and frequency; distinctions are made between recognized and non-recognized political parties. Political ads must be clearly identified for what they are. These controls are considered necessary; they prevent undue influence of one philosophy over another. The same type of control should be exercised over all lifestyle advertising (including of course, ads preaching the wisdom of conservation).

Corporate advertising can also be overtly political. In the United States, Texaco ran a commercial which argued against any effort to break up the big oil companies into smaller units. The Federal Communication Commission, recognizing that fair play was being jeopardized by corporate propaganda, ordered a television station to give a public interest lobby equal time to present its opposite perspective. One counter ad showed the oil business wringing dollars out of a map of the United States. Another showed oil executives playing Monopoly with uncontrollable greed. In a third an Arab mugged an American with a gas pump nozzle. The Arab then took off his robes to reveal an oil executive.

An equal-time policy such as this—though open to excesses of its own—would act as an effective deterrent to overt political interference. It could also be used to present other points of view for potentially dangerous products (such as certain non-prescription drugs) or particularly useless products (such as certain breakfast cereals). Equal-time provisions, particularly when exercised in the offending ad, would also check misleading advertising.

Warner-Lambert, a large pharmaceutical company, was forced to spend $10 million in advertising correcting the wrong impression it had created over time as to Listerine's qualities. Had an equal-time policy existed, this would not have been necessary. The wrong impression would never have been successfully conveyed.

Products known to be harmful, such as cigarettes, should not be allowed to be advertised at all, even if for various reasons their production is allowed.

Equal-time provisions might also be used to counter impressions made by institutional advertising—advertising supporting not a specific product but the organization behind it. The good will this kind of advertising creates tends to make the consumer more loyal and less critical. He becomes more susceptible to a bad decision, one based on a company's image rather than its products' qualities.

If a company's intention is to inform its public, the company shouldn't object to giving a balanced view. Part of its institutional ad could be devoted to an opposing perspective. An organization not willing to subject itself to such scrutiny need not advertise on this basis. But in the court of public opinion, it should be open to cross-examination.

In theory, there appear to be delicate but dangerous obstacles to advocacy advertising: to whom goes the privilege of presenting the other point of view, what happens when several different interests wish to oppose an ad, and other questions of fair play seem to make the cure more questionable than the sickness. In practice, though, these problems would not ordinarily exist. Battle lines are usually drawn well before ideas have advanced to the stage they are publicly promoted. In the consumer field, for example, there is a wide consensus that the Consumers Association of Canada would be more than competent to comment on dubious products put forth by manufacturers. In the energy field, where there are several strong public interest groups in Canada, all cooperate with each other.

But in those cases where there are true conflicts of interest, the onus should not be on the advertiser. If the opposing perspectives can't agree among themselves on how to counter an ad they oppose (not too likely since they would be at least unified in that), the ad could appear unopposed.

Very few ads would need advocacy advertising at all. With advertisers aware that any extravagant claim would now be challenged, advertising would become more responsible. Advertisers and their adversaries could even declare a détente and agree on ad content before ads are produced.

Not all non-informative ads advocate a lifestyle, or present an overt political preference or promote an institution's public image. Many have simply nothing to say. An ad such as this, an ad which has nothing to say, does not fulfill the accepted purpose of an ad, which is to inform. It should not be classed as an ad. It may be an art form; and it may have value as that, but it doesn't have value as an ad.

A conserver society may decide to require that all ads have information value, and to make that information the thrust of the ad. (Otherwise those clever advertisers could frustrate the spirit of that requirement by sprinkling senseless ads with gratuitous information, much as pornographers punctuate their product with platitudes to give them redeeming social value.)

At the very least, all ads and all promotion not performing the direct business function of informing the consumer should not be considered legitimate business expenses. A company can presently write off any advertising expenditure as profitably as if it made an equal contribution to charity. Losing this tax status would effectively double the cost of non-informative advertising, perhaps eliminating it in the process. Eliminated, too, might be those products with nothing to offer.

The influence of marketing is more insidious than merely the misinformation or non-information of the consumer. To a large extent, when an ad foists itself upon us, we are alerted that we're about to have our credulity strained. Whether we accept the message or not, we know we've been exposed to a self-serving device.

Not so with marketing's behind-the-scenes machinations. In a massive indirect sell, the advertising industry enlists the help of whomever it can reach. In the pharmaceutical business, over $1 billion is spent annually in the United States persuading physicians what drugs their patients need. That figure, $1 billion, represents more than three times the total annual budget of all American medical schools. It represents $1 out of every $1,000 in the Gross National Product.

So it is elsewhere. The disc jockey is encouraged to promote the right records, the grocer to stock the right sardines, the hairdresser to sell the right shampoo. And through it all, those who cooperate with the ad men are wined and dined, bribed with free samples and free trips to conventions.

When a doctor passes along a sample to a patient, only a cynic would question the forces that brought it to him. A stronger endorsement doesn't exist. Faith in hairdressers and disc jockeys may not be as high as in doctors but they'll do for the advertiser's purposes.

Perhaps the most insidious forms of promotion are those that seem the most innocent. Those cars our screen stars step out of and the clothes they step into are often provided free of charge by their respective manufacturers. In exchange manufacturers receive a credit at the end of the show and exposure throughout it—exposure that can be more potent than paid lifestyle advertising in influencing an admiring audience.

Bribes, whether outright in the form of graft, rationalized in the form of free samples, or camouflaged in the form of loans to movies and television shows, are currently charged up as promotional expenses. Yet they do not provide a direct or legitimate business function. They should not be considered legitimate business expenses; they should not be subject to tax advantages.

Unnecessary packaging requires similar taxation policies. The purpose of packaging is to protect and contain its contents. It can extend to labelling and instructions on the use of the contents. But when packaging becomes part of the selling mechanism, it must be considered in the same light as advertising. Over-packaging may be pretty, but it isn't packaging—it is non-informative advertising. It, too, doesn't deserve the tax break it's been getting.

These taxation measures do not require a fundamental change in policy; they would only be making present policies consistent. It is possible, however, that taxation measures won't be enough. Companies may be prepared to absorb these increased costs to create wants, or they may be able to pass on these costs to the consumer.

A conserver society may require the elimination of marketing practices that aren't consistent with marketing principles. It may provide incentives for competing industries to negotiate an absolute reduction in advertising. When markets can't be increased and advertising only spurs a see-saw war for a share of the market, little is to be gained. The savings all the firms would realize could be partly passed on to the consumer, partly kept as profit.

Reform of the advertising system (a return from its baser instincts to its basic principles) would signal a return to traditional democratic principles. With advertising capital shifting to informative advertising, the information the consumer receives will be free from much of the distortion that previously clouded his judgment. Wants will no longer be created on the same scale, and this will be accompanied by a reduction of the production which exists for these wants.

This productive capability can shift to arenas where it will be more usefully deployed, or the capital which it would require can be distributed elsewhere for other purposes. The bogus competition based on imaginary distinctions between products can be diverted to competition based on quality and price. It would mark a step back from monopolistic policies, a step toward the free enterprise system.

Once the negative effects of advertising are in tow, and we begin to conserve our capital for more essential ends, we will have the means to systematically start eradicating our three persisting, seemingly insoluble economic woes: our foreign debt, inflation, and unemployment.

PART FOUR

Solving the Unsolvable

15 *Conservation of Capital*

WHEN JEAN CHRETIEN was Minister of Industry, Trade and Commerce, he understood clearly that Canadians should spend more money to stimulate the economy. When he first became Minister of Finance he still understood this, but also came to understand that Canadians should save more money. As he became more familiar with the Ministry of Finance and less familiar with his training in the Trade and Commerce portfolio, Jean Chrétien understood clearly that, above all, Canadians should save more money.

There are those who feel Mr. Chrétien's positions were inconsistent. After all, they note, he did take diametrically opposed stances. But Mr. Chrétien's comments can also be seen as being completely consistent—not with each other but with the historic positions of his respective portfolios. In his function as Industry, Trade and Commerce Minister, Mr. Chrétien's plea for increased spending accurately represented the predominant views of the business community. Business experts interested in increasing their own business tend to call for the public to participate in bettering their lot.

The Ministry of Finance, however, has as its constituency the financial community. These people—our financial analysts, investment dealers, economists, and bankers—tend to think in terms of the economy as a whole. They are not so much preoccupied with immediate profits as they are with the ability of the economy to sustain itself over a long period of time. To do this the economy needs to invest in capital with which to maintain and expand its productive ability. This investment capital can only come from our society's savings. (Whether we invest our savings, or let our banks and other financial institutions do it, most savings end up as investments.)

There are two kinds of capital: physical capital (actual goods) and financial capital (money). Financial capital can be paper money or a bank account, it can be credits and claims written on a piece of paper, or exist as stocks and bonds. Through the process of lending and borrowing it can help create physical capital but it is not physical capital in itself. It merely represents physical capital.

Financial capital is worth more than the paper it's printed on when its holder can exchange it for physical capital. Many people holding a $100 bill would expect to be able to purchase $100 worth of merchandise with it. When too much financial capital is created as, for example, when a country prints too much money, causing inflation, it takes more financial capital to purchase the same amount of merchandise. Physical capital goods haven't been created in the process, although financial capital has.

Physical capital is equipment and buildings, nickel mines and waterfalls, farms and forests, schools and hospitals. To create it requires the right combination of materials and workers. If a shortage of physical capital exists, printing money, or borrowing it from other countries, will not increase our domestic supply of steel and cement, or steelworkers, or construction foremen. Borrowed money can be used to import needed physical capital, but then it must be repaid, with interest, from our future stocks of physical capital (our future savings). The net gain for Canada would be, at least partially, nullified.

When financial capital is borrowed from abroad to pay for our present consumption, it doesn't increase our physical capital at all. For if that money is to pay for, say, oil consumption, it cannot at the same time pay for physical capital.

The bulk of the capital for Canada's future needs must come from our own savings—the savings of our corporations, individuals and governments. Because, as a general rule, countries which rank higher in their rate of savings also rank higher in their annual growth rate, every financial expert from the Prime Minister on down traditionally encourages the habit.

In times of particular stress, the encouragement becomes particularly eloquent, and can even come from business quarters. Their comments have come to sound like a refrain, such as the chairman of Imperial Oil's tireless reiteration of "Canada must divert more income into activities that promote production and less into areas that merely stimulate consumption, if living standards are to be maintained. While we have been insisting on getting more and more out of our economy, we have been putting less and less into it." And the president of the Investment Dealers Association of Canada's poetic announcement that "the picture is not improving." And Prime Minister Trudeau's profound explanation that Canadians are "soft" and "living beyond their means."

The savings these gentlemen would like to see can only be easily achieved by Canadians thinking more about their purchases: relying on more durable goods and wasting less of what they use—exactly what a conserver society would propose. But if they spoke in specifics and recommended that Canadians cut back on consumption of certain cars, cake mixes, and cosmetics it would appear neither political nor businesslike. Not able to spell out how to consume less, they content themselves with the euphemism "save more."

When a person decides to save money, say by putting it into a bank that pays 7% interest, he will benefit by that amount. The bank will turn around and lend that money at 9% or 10% interest, giving itself a profit in the process. The borrower of that money, say a corporation, can invest it in capital equipment that might bring it 20% or 30% or 40% return on that investment. The members of this small society are all prospering. Their individual decisions seem to be leading to the welfare of the group.

Yet the members of this society are very much dependent on each other. If the corporation doesn't achieve a good rate of return it may not be able to repay its loan to the bank, which, in turn, may not be able to return the individual's money and go bankrupt (in which event in Canada, even if the bank goes bankrupt, the individual's deposits are insured by the federal government). If the individual doesn't decide to save the money he won't receive the 7% interest, and the bank won't be able to take his money and loan it to some other member of society. The bank won't make its 2% or 3% profit and the corporation that might have borrowed it won't realize its 20% or 30% or 40% rate of return (unless it can find the capital it needs elsewhere).

The decision of the individual not to earn 7% interest affects the rest of society. While the decision should stay his alone, it won't be his to make until he pays his own way—until others aren't affected by it. In an interdependent economy he will be responsible for his actions. Whatever he takes away from a society's well-being through his free choice he should be prepared to put back.

When Canada's domestic savings aren't enough to meet its capital requirements, it tries to borrow from foreign markets. The interest on foreign money may be the same as the interest on Canadian funds, but when the interest is paid outside the country it is money lost to our economy. An individual, or a corporation, or a government that doesn't save adequately should be responsible for the interest on that part of his consumption which could have been saved. This way the rest of society will not be paying for decisions he made that adversely affect it.

All money is either saved or spent. Since this interest will be applied only to money which is spent the interest can be thought of as a sales tax, but one that discriminates between products that promote saving and products that don't.

Take the example of two electric can openers, each costing $10. One lasts two years, the other five. The one that lasts two years costs $5 per year; the more durable one costs $2 per year. The amount of money that a purchaser of the less durable one is not saving is $3 per year, and since the can opener is expected to last for two years the amount not saved on the purchase is $6. Because this $6 is not being saved, it will have to be borrowed at a cost of perhaps 10% (if that's the foreign interest rate) or 60 cents. A sales tax equal to that amount (possibly replacing present sales taxes) would suffice to compensate society.

The can opener that is most durable would have no sales tax levied, for as long as it remained most durable. Should other can openers be marketed, their durability (or life-cycle costs) would all be judged in comparison to the most durable one, and, conceivably, they could all have different sales taxes. (To avoid complicating normal purchases, this tax could be collected from the manufacturer, the way federal sales taxes are paid without retail customers participating directly.)

This principle can be applied to non-durable goods and services as well. Food, for example, might be sales taxed based on its nutritional value; repair shops based on the length of warranty they offer.

Although this would in no way limit the ability of a purchaser to exercise his free will, it would emphasize the advantages in purchasing with saving in mind, perhaps encouraging the thrifty habits so desired by our financial experts. And it would allow those not concerned with saving to act as they choose without burdening the rest of society.

Traditional economists may have said it wouldn't occur, but the entire world is suffering from a severe capital shortage. President Ford and other patriotic Americans wanted to launch "Project Independence"—a plan to make the U.S. self-sufficient in energy. They placed a high priority on freeing their country from another threat of blackmail, yet had to abandon the plan when they realized the project would require 75% of all available capital between 1975 and 1980 to be diverted to the energy sector of the U.S. economy.

Even without Project Independence, the United States faces a tough time. Former Treasury Secretary William Simon estimated America's capital shortage for the ten years ending in 1985 would total $1 trillion. World-wide, industrialized countries are agonizing over where to place the scarce supplies of capital they can muster. No longer able to tackle all problems at once, they must balance their allocation of resources between the public and private sector, between energy and minerals extractions and between competing industrial sectors.

In a capital-short world, the problems for Canada become particularly acute. The Canadian economy is inherently capital-intensive. Because of our geography, we face capital costs in transportation and communication of a magnitude unknown to most other nations. Because of our large seasonal climatic variations, the massive capital costs needed to handle large seasonal peak loads in heating, transportation, and other sectors are unavoidable. Our need for capital is also exacerbated by our present reliance on primary resource industries. Development of the north is another problem—creating one job there can cost more than $1 million in capital investments.

Not surprisingly, it is becoming increasingly difficult for Canada to meet its capital needs. Four times as much capital could be required in the next decade as was required in the last. This requirement—estimated at $900 billion—could make competition for capital more severe, and the need to allocate it fairly more stringent, than ever before.

At one time any bank—even any person—had the right to create money and other forms of financial capital. There were positive and negative features to this right but after the Great Depression—when the negative features seemed to predominate—governments stepped in and began controlling financial activities as never before. As a result, the financial industry is now highly regulated: currencies are very carefully controlled and even bank use of money is subject to strict supervision.

Fear of inflation forces printing foremen at the nations' mints to slow increases in the supply of new paper money; supposedly in relation to increases in the supply of new physical capital. At any given moment there is a finite supply of physical capital in a country or in the world, and a correspondingly (though not equal) finite supply of financial capital. It is the physical capital the investors are bidding for, but they use the financial capital with which to make the bids.

Since there is a limited amount of capital, and so many who want it to go to them, it isn't always distributed fairly. Big borrowers, such as large corporations and government utilities, negotiate favourable interest rates for themselves. They receive preferential rates because they are good risks and because they borrow a lot. Once these borrowers have taken their share of the available capital (more than half), the smaller borrowers are left to bid for the remaining capital, which is now scarcer than before. This shortage of supply and large demand raises the price of the remaining capital for the remaining borrowers. They now have to pay a larger interest rate for its use.

Had the big borrowers borrowed more, leaving less for the small borrowers, the price to the small borrowers would have been even higher. Had the big borrowers borrowed less, the price to the small borrowers would have been less.

The capital, a commodity artificially controlled by governments, a commodity that should not be entirely subject to the laws of supply and demand, ends up being allocated on precisely this basis. By making big money cheaper to get than small amounts, the system artificially favours big money, capital-intensive projects at the expense of small projects, which now become artificially expensive. Capital-intensive projects have their place, but so do more modest endeavours.

Since Canada's is a free economy, all sectors of our economy should have equal access to the available stocks of capital. Those that require larger amounts of scarce capital could compensate by paying progressively larger interest rates on loans. This would tend to make them more efficient in deciding the minimum amount of capital they require while allowing the base interest rate to be lowered for themselves and smaller borrowers. The rate structure could allow many big borrowers to pay the same overall amount in interest while freeing money, at lower rates, for the small borrowers.

As an example, instead of a company borrowing $100 million at a flat 9% interest, it might pay 5% for the first $100,000, 6% for the next $1 million, 7% for the next $10 million, 8% for the next $25 million, 9% for the following $25 million, 10% for the $25 million after that, and 11% for the balance. The company's total interest payment would be virtually the same, but having the rates skewed this way would provide an incentive for finding solutions requiring less capital. When that happens, the capital that isn't borrowed becomes available for other borrowers. Big borrowers that continue to require a disproportionate share of capital would pay an increasingly higher interest rate for the privilege of using their disproportionate share.

Interest rates vary with the risk in lending, and lending institutions need not abandon charging higher rates for riskier ventures. In fact, they need not change their practices at all. Rather than regulating the interest on loans as they're made, this bookkeeping could conveniently take place after all the loans are in and a company prepares its annual audit. At that time all loans could be tallied, appropriate interest rates assigned, and appropriate amounts credited or debited as required.

Corporations that do not need to borrow money, and there are many of them, do not hurt the borrowing rate of others. These companies, companies like Kodak and many oil firms, have been so successful that their profits alone have been able to finance almost all their capital requirements. As long as this remains the case, as long as they continue to rely on their own resources, they would be able to use their capital as they see fit, in large projects or small, without paying a premium for the privilege.

Spreading capital and removing the bias against small borrowers by giving them the same rate structure as large borrowers would restore the vitality of capital markets and reduce tendencies to overinvest.

This would conserve capital.

Making an inefficient purchase more costly by adding a sales tax to the purchase price would compensate society to the exact degree the purchase hurts society, and inspire people to pick out more prudent products.

This would also conserve capital.

Once we have a society geared to conserving capital we could begin to dig ourselves out of the deepest hole any society, in any part of the world, has ever freely dug itself into. We could begin to get out from under the burden of the largest international debt in the history of mankind.

16 *Retiring the Foreign Debt*

EVERY MINUTE CANADA'S national debt increases by about $15,000. In one hour, it's up by close to $1 million, and in a day by over $20 million. In 1965, the interest on the national debt amounted to $1.1 billion a year. By 1970, it had risen to $1.8 billion. By 1975 the annual interest payments on the national debt exceeded $3.7 billion. Since 1971, the federal government has been spending more for interest on this debt than for national defence. It now costs more than old age pensions, more than family allowance and medicare combined. The national debt costs the federal government more than any other single expenditure.

Besides the national debt, Canadians are privileged to pay provincial and municipal debts. By 1977, all government debts equalled 65% of the Gross National Product, totalling $120 billion—$12,500 for every employed person or $5,200 for every man, woman, and child in the country. The cost of servicing these debts, close to $9 billion per year, represented $822.92 per employed person, more than twice the cost five years earlier.

In only one year of the last 15 did the federal government pay off more in old debts than it accumulated in new debts. The last year in which the provinces paid off more than they borrowed was 1946. Net government debt has gone up almost every year since the end of World War II. To pay it off the country's population would have to work full-time for over a year, all the while turning over all its pay cheques to governments.

Our governments are unlikely to suggest we do this. Instead, to pay for old debts, they incur new debts. As the debts add up new loans become harder to find. Lending sources at home begin to get exhausted and funds are found in foreign countries.

When these foreign funds are used to finance an expansion of the economy, the ramifications for the country are not necessarily serious: that expansion will eventually generate the money to repay these loans. But when foreign funds are used to pay for consumption at home they don't contribute to the country's ability to repay them. The ramifications here can be disastrous.

In 1945, Canada owed investors in other countries $4.2 billion. This debt grew to be about eight times as great—$32.4 billion—by 1973. Between 1974 and 1976 another $13.5 billion was added. (At this stage Canada was borrowing outside the country more than twice as much as the world's next heaviest borrower, Brazil.) Another $9 billion was added to our foreign debt by the end of 1977, bringing the total outstanding to about $54.5 billion. By 1978, the debt exceeded the $60 billion level. It took Canada only five years to amass a volume of foreign debt equal to the combined debts accumulated in the first 100 years of Confederation. We are more in debt than any other nation on earth. Our debts total more than half the foreign debts of all the underdeveloped nations combined, nations having more than half the world's population.

At any one time in history, there have been only a few creditor countries (countries that lend more than they borrow), and these countries have been responsible for most of the capital which has been invested throughout the world. In the latter part of the nineteenth century and on into the twentieth the leading source of capital was Great Britain, regarded as the classic example of a creditor country. Although British investments had ceased to grow by the beginning of World War II, it was still the largest lender. The next largest lender at that time was the United States, whose level of lending was less than half Britain's. Belgium, France, the Netherlands, and Switzerland (other industrialized nations) were the other prominent creditor countries.

The debtor countries were principally the primary producing colonial countries—Canada, Australia, India, China, and the Dutch East Indies. Canada's debt was much larger than any of the others.

The war changed the world financial order. Most of the European countries, faced with massive war debts, lost their creditor status. Britain's war-time indebtedness forced it to liquidate its holdings in Canada and various other countries, starting a slide from which it has never recovered. Although Britain remained a creditor country for more than a decade, the United States emerged as the leading creditor after the war. And its leading debtor has been Canada.

In the postwar years, more than one third of United States private investment has been in Canada, more than in any other single nation, more than in all of Latin America (the next largest region of investments), and more than in all the countries of the world outside the Americas combined. Canada's foreign debt now amounts to more than a quarter of our entire GNP. The interest on that debt—under $700 million a year in 1974—now increases by between $1 billion and $2 billion a year. The capital leaving Canada by 1980 will exceed $5 billion a year in interest payments alone. We already find ourselves in the compromised position of having to borrow money abroad just to repay the interest on past borrowings.

If the situation continues to deteriorate it could threaten our sovereignty. As Britain and other heavily indebted nations have found out, the terms for foreign loans become partial management of national economies by foreign banks or lending institutions. Even our foreign policy could become compromised or constrained (if it hasn't already) by excessive foreign debts, particularly to the United States.

Our foreign debts arise from importing more goods and services than we export. It is this difference we owe, and this difference we pay interest on (other factors that contribute to the foreign debt, such as borrowing money from abroad, are really just other forms of importing more goods and services than we export. The foreign money that is borrowed is used to buy foreign goods, and when the debt is later repaid with Canadian dollars, those dollars are used by the foreign country to purchase Canadian goods).

To reduce our debt, we must export more than we import. This is normally done by either raising the amount of our exports or reducing the amount of our imports (or a combination of the two). Canada has adopted a third course. Not only do we try to export our goods and services but, with the discovery that the goose that lays the golden eggs fetches a better price than the eggs, we also sell off our assets—the companies that produce our goods. In our vigilant attempts to get out from under debt, we've sold off two thirds of all our industries.

The result has been to make Canada unique on two counts: we are both the most heavily indebted nation on earth and the only one whose industry is so substantially dominated by foreigners.

In the last half century we have run a steady deficit in the export of services (such as tourism and consulting fees) in every year but three. For the decade ending 1974, the deficit accumulated at the rate of about $2 billion a year. It has since risen, reaching $7.64 billion in 1977, and is expected to top $10 billion by 1980.

Partly off-setting our steady deficit in services has been a steady surplus in the export of goods. But to raise our exports of goods to the point where we could start making a dent in the foreign debt we would have to triple our best performance ever ($3 billion in 1970). By 1979 it would take more than $9 billion to offset our deficit in services—unrealistic by anyone's standards.

And since almost every politician, and almost every economic body, finds the problem so unmanageable, it is largely ignored. The dollar is allowed to float and economists try to "fine-tune" the economy. Comments are made by our financial leaders of the need to work harder, and by our politicians that we're living beyond our means. And there it rests. Aside from hopes our economy will pick up when the world economy picks up, or hopes we'll hit it lucky the way the British did with their North Sea oil, or hopes we'll soon have access to new foreign markets, an air of resignation reigns over our economic centres.

Although Canada traditionally has a surplus in the goods we export (currently about $2 billion), that surplus comes from the sale of our primary goods—mainly our minerals and our wheat. These primary goods (and associated processes) account for about $13 billion. Offsetting them is a $11 billion deficit in finished goods (manufactured goods) resulting in the $2 billion figure. Since 1970, Canada's trade deficit in finished goods has increased steadily as a percentage of GNP while we've increasingly specialized in the export of primary raw materials. A conserver society could reverse these trends.

Rather than continuing to fall back on our primary resources to pay for a larger and larger share of our nation's income, we should begin to conserve these resources by cutting back on exports until we are both certain we have enough to meet our own long-term needs and confident we are getting their full value in a resource-short world. This does not necessarily imply that our resources will become smaller money earners. In 1973 and 1974, when the world-wide shortage of resources drove prices up steeply in primary and processed products (which we export) while the prices of manufactured goods (which we import) stayed more stable, Canada was able to sell less and earn more. The shortages could become increasingly severe as world economies discover they are impinging on decreasing, easily accessible supplies. With increasing shortages will come increasing prices that will in turn facilitate our conservation goals.

But these price increases would not be necessary to phase in conserver policies. With the conservation of capital principle at work, much of the planned obsolescence dragging down our economy would be eliminated. The true, total costs of all products and services would become known, allowing individuals to make informed decisions on the purchases they want while encouraging manufacturers to produce for those wants. Artificial advantages helping companies produce wasteful products would be removed, and those wishing to be inefficient would be compensating society for the added burden they'd be placing on others. The more efficient a product, the less it would be taxed, offering consumers a double advantage when deciding to conserve our capital.

If we needed just 10% fewer lightbulbs and just 10% fewer ashtrays; if cars lasted just 10% longer and got just 10% better mileage, if our TV sets were repaired to last just 10% longer and we could do without just 10% of our advertising and 10% of our bureaucrats—if we could do just 10% better overall than we have been doing—the savings overall to the economy would be about $20 billion a year. In three years we would be able to eliminate our foreign debt. By the fourth year we could become an exporter of capital—a creditor country.

For a conventional economy a 10% saving of this kind represents a monumental undertaking. Aside from war-time periods, Canada has rarely been able to save enough to reduce our foreign debt. If a conserver society were in place, savings of a mere 10% would be considered modest—a conserver society would not set its sights so low.

But even at a 10% efficiency improvement, the balance of trade would swing in Canada's favour to a much greater extent than a rate of $20 billion a year. With products having their efficiencies based on Canadian standards, manufacturers who specialize in meeting Canadian requirements would have natural advantages in selling to Canadians. These manufacturers would, as a matter of course, be Canadian manufacturers. Imports would become less useful for our needs once our revitalized manufacturing sector developed products and processes of its own, distinctively designed to meet specialized needs. These designs could find applications world wide, turning our present $11 billion deficit in finished goods into a surplus as we mature as an industrialized nation.

Canadians have often been proud that foreign countries find us a good place to invest. Our ability to attract foreign capital seems to some as somehow a tribute or sign of success. Foreign investment and foreign debt, because of this prevailing attitude, seem part of the process of industrial expansion. But rapid industrial development and the rapid increase in production generate huge amounts of surplus capital, and industrial success is usually accompanied by an increase in foreign assets.

Affluent nations are not capital importers but capital exporters. The United States, West Germany, Sweden, Switzerland, Japan—industrialized nations Canada has long tried to emulate —all are creditor nations.

17 *Taking the Wind Out of Inflation*

IN THE DAYS when money was worth its weight in gold or silver or copper coins inflation was simple to understand. When the metal content in coins was reduced it took more to purchase the same ancient good or service. That was inflation.

Individuals who took it upon themselves to devalue coins, say by shaving them and selling the scraps, were engaging in theft and properly punished by their rulers. Rulers who decided to reduce the amount of metal in their coins, or run in some cheaper brass in the hope no one would notice, were exempt from any such recriminations. Unlike the thieves the rulers invariably had loftier motives; usually the extra money made was spent on their own greater glorification, or to finance a war.

The decline and fall of the Roman Empire is attributed by some to inflation. To finance the expensive Punic Wars Romans started stretching their currency supplies by having the mint modify its coin-making recipe. So successful was this that Roman coins continued to be steadily debased after the wars to finance other projects. By the time of Aurelian the basic silver coin contained 95% copper. Later its silver content was brought down to 2%.

It used to be that the supply of valuable metals (and so coins) increased in rough proportion to the supply of other goods. This kept the purchasing power of money more or less steady. When the Romans (among others) changed this balance by putting far more money into circulation, so that there was more money than the goods that the money could buy, buyers had to bid higher for the goods than before. And the price went up.

Inflation became a trickier concept to understand after 1492. Christopher Columbus was the culprit. His discovery of the Americas set in motion a vast flow of precious metals from the sadly unexploited mines of the Incas, Aztecs, and Indians. The good that was wrought by providing local employment for these native peoples in their own mines was offset to some degree by the effect all their treasures had on the people of Europe. They drove prices up.

The price increases were first noticed in Spain, where the metals first arrived. Between 1500 and 1600, prices rose five-fold. As the treasures travelled to other parts of Europe (through trade and theft) inflation travelled with them. Prices in Britain rose two-and-a-half times within a century of Co-lumbus' discovery, and three-and-a-half times by the 1670s.

This inflation was not caused by a debasing of the currency, as inflation in Roman times was, but it was nevertheless based on the same principle. More new money (made from the in-flow of metals) was put into circulation than new goods. Al-though the money may have been of almost pure metal, it became worth less because so much of it was available. Rela-tive to the metal, goods became more scarce, and more valua-ble. It now took more money to buy these scarcities.

But inflation of the post-Columbus variety is far less com-mon than inflation of the Roman kind. After the 1630s, when the richest ore in the silver mines of Mexico was exhausted, exports of silver (by far the most abundant of the precious raw resources of the day) dropped off. Spain's main pursuit, though, and the main pursuit of the other European nations continued. This pursuit was war. Whether a hobby or the habit of the times, war was the accepted sponge for two thirds of all the revenues of all the warring nations. Such devotion to this pastime ultimately led to the need for more money, and rulers once more saw the Roman advantage in cheapening the value of money.

But by then paper money had become the vogue. As paper

is more plentiful than the cheapest of metals, it opened up untold opportunities for increasing the supply of money and with it, inflation. But though the game may have changed, the rules stayed the same. The price of goods (the price of supply) varied with the amount of money in circulation (the amount of demand).

This is the famous principle of supply and demand, a principle so dominant in economic thought that it applies equally when determining the price of a real commodity (such as a house or a hamburger) or the price of a fictitious commodity (such as currency, which only represents real commodities). In a free market, the price of any commodity will tend to increase as more people demand it. To decrease the price, the demand for it (relative to supply) must be reduced. This can be accomplished by either making more of the commodity (increasing the supply to lower the price. Traditionally this is accompanied by higher employment); or by putting it out of the reach of more people (decreasing the amount of money in circulation to lower the demand). Traditionally unemployment rises as a result.

Modern economies have been unable to make either method work. Inflation, normally the companion of war, civil disorder, famine or other catastrophe has acquired new habits. It now persists in periods of rising prosperity as well. Inflation has become integrated into our industrial society.

Part of the reason is we no longer have a free economy. The free market has become subject to the whims of big business and we have become subject to the control of advertising.

Increasing supply in order to lower prices has become an impossibility. Increased production results in additional wages and other monies paid out because of it, increasing purchasing power. If this increased ability to buy was left alone, inflation would not be a necessary consequence. Those who wanted something would get it; those who didn't wouldn't. But because of the marvels of modern advertising, wants are created where wants don't already exist. These created wants are not independent of production. They exist because of the production. Demand is kept at insatiable levels and can never be met as long as advertising succeeds in interfering with free market choices.

In an economy that is responsive to the forces of the marketplace, producers try to maximize profits. Ideally, they are wringing every last cent out of their customers. If they charge too much, sales will drop. If they charge too little, they're losing profits. It is the free market that tells them exactly how much to charge, exactly what the traffic will bear. The market sets the price, and as demand rises and falls, so will the market price. But to the large corporation, money isn't everything. Although the market might allow it to raise its price, the corporation won't do so on the market's say-so. It has its own reasons.

The corporation might be afraid of public reaction to a price hike; it may want to first make sure the rest of the industry will raise its price too. The corporation could be concerned that, over a longer span of time, the price increases will be damaging to the competitive position of the company or the industry, or it might be afraid raising prices will rouse unions into making disruptive wage demands.

Big companies think in terms of their own long-term security. Short-run gains can conflict with their ultimate self-interest, and, since they're large enough to resist market forces, they wisely do. In contrast to the small private sector, where prices rise or drop as demand dictates, companies in the big private sector raise prices when it suits them. They are largely independent of the market, which also makes them largely independent of government attempts to decrease demand by decreasing purchasing power.

Governments try to decrease demand through fiscal or monetary policy. Traditional monetary policy in the face of inflation raises interest rates and generally makes it more expensive for consumers and business to borrow money. This slows the rate at which new money is put into circulation (literally it slows down the mint's printing presses). Fiscal policy tries to achieve the same end—remove some of the money from circulation—by the government refusing to spend the money it has taxed.

In a free market, either method would be expected to work. But in a market where most of industry is concentrated in few hands, big business can decide to raise prices even when the government tries to lower demand by taking money out of circulation. Inflationary price increases can take place while deflationary policies are being conducted. All companies need is the right opportunity to raise prices.

Enter the unions. Inflationary times lead to union demands for increased wages. Typically, after corporations grant a wage hike they announce a price hike for their products that's even greater. Of course, they could have raised their prices to the same level without the wage increases. The wage increases did nothing to convince customers their higher-priced products were worth the price. They only provided the excuse the corporation needed to implement a price increase it was ready to implement.

Price increases for primary products—almost all produced by large firms—affect a lot of products at the same time. These across-the-board increases are felt by the economy as a whole, and stimulate other wage demands to compensate for the inflationary rises in price. When these wage demands are met there are further price hikes, and the inflationary wage-price spiral is well on its way.

It used to be part of the conventional wisdom that inflation could only occur when demand was high. When plants are working to capacity and the labour force is fully productive they are supplying all the goods they can. If there's a demand for more goods than can be supplied, prices will rise. The solution to inflation was to throw part of the labour force out of work. This would both reduce the ability of plants to work to capacity and impoverish the workers, giving them less money with which to demand goods. When unemployment became high the solution was to print more money and pass it around. The money gave people added purchasing power, and convinced companies it was time to produce goods to benefit by it. To produce the goods they hired the unemployed, eliminating the unemployment problem.

The choice was always between inflation and unemployment. It was not thought possible to have both at the same time.

Canada now has extraordinarily high inflation coupled with extraordinarily high unemployment. To complete the mystery, 20% of the country's industrial capacity is shut down. Traditional economics has no answers. Traditional economics did not anticipate the costs that were going to catch up to us, costs only a conserver society could have dealt with.

At one time, anyone with the right backyard in Texas could dig a hole in the ground and strike oil. Oil was cheap to extract. Today we have to look for oil in the backyards of Eskimos. When we find it we have to figure out how to get it out of the Arctic in a way that won't destroy the environment. We have to develop technologies for digging into ocean floors and coping with calamitous climatic conditions. All this takes money, and it makes our oil expensive. It isn't expensive because of the amount of money in circulation in the economy or because our fiscal or monetary policy is letting us down. The oil is expensive because, relative to everything else, it actually costs more.

The Organization of Petroleum Exporting Countries (OPEC), and the Arab countries that dominate it, is often blamed for triggering the long period of inflation the world is currently experiencing. Yet OPEC only raised the price of its oil to a price that is still considerably cheaper than the cost of our new oil.

If we had a cheaper replacement we wouldn't buy it. OPEC's oil is still, if anything, underpriced. The world markets would pay more for it. All OPEC needs (like other large organizations that control an industry) is an excuse to raise it further. The excuses will come and oil price rises will continue to have inflationary effects.

Five years after the dramatic OPEC price hike and the reeling inflation it helped set off, the world is still plagued by rates of inflation much greater than before OPEC. The price increases have had their chance to work through our economic systems, and these systems would normally have long ago absorbed the shocks and settled down, if it were only the oil hike that was responsible.

In fact, what happened to the price of oil has been happening to some extent to the price of our other non-renewable resources. Whether iron or copper or nickel or lead, they are getting more expensive to extract. We've used up most of our high-grade ores, ores that were easy to find. Now we're working with lower-grade ores and going further and further afield in search of new deposits. This takes more and more capital—in transportation costs, in developing new technologies and in more sophisticated equipment. As long as we're in the situation where we're running out of resources, inflation will be one of the costs we'll have to pay.

Hurtling more and more capital into retrieval of resources and getting less and less back for our investment will pre-empt other more realistic options. We will pay in higher interest rates today and in lost flexibility tomorrow. Capital is in such short supply that competition for it is becoming increasingly intense, raising interest rates and limiting those who have access to capital. In the energy field, where by far the biggest chunk of scarce capital is spent, almost all the money has been going to the development of conventional energy sources like oil and nuclear. To get energy from these sources, huge amounts of energy must be wasted. It takes millions of barrels of oil to crush the rocks and heat and retort the shale and sands, not to mention refining and transportation. The net energy gained is only a fraction of the total theoretically available.

With almost all capital available for energy being sunk irretrievably into closed options like nuclear, the wide range of renewable energy options has been pre-empted. Should the nuclear experiment not pay off, the cost of this lost flexibility will become painfully evident in the future. If our overdependence on this one source of energy proves untenable—because it isn't economical to maintain necessary health or safety standards, because the social problems associated with nuclear are too severe, or because the environmental costs of increased levels of radioactivity are too high—the costs will show up as future inflation, just as previous social and environmental costs are showing up as present inflation.

The growth of industrialized society brought a wealth of goods. Consumers were not hesitant to pay for these goods, but they were hesitant to pay for some of the costs associated with these goods. A car was paid for cheerfully but paying the taxes that provided it with smooth roads drew complaints. Few regretted the private insurance payments that protected private property but when policemen and firemen (without whom private insurers would not so willingly have offered protection) demanded raises they were despised for selfish social conduct.

Our unwillingness to pay for anything we can avoid was no less evident in the business community. Products were made without concern for the poisons discharged into our environment. And they were sold without concern for the safety of the people who bought them. This has significantly raised health costs—now the largest component of our government budget. And the direct costs alone of cleaning up the environment are approaching 2% of our country's entire output in goods and services.

The mounting costs we've been experiencing result from our failure to do things properly the first time. There are now more old cars being recalled annually than new cars manufactured. It is cheaper to recall them than to allow the costs in human injury and property damage that would otherwise result. But it would have been cheapest of all to have taken the time to design the cars well in the first place. Part of the price tag of all our goods and services now contains a component for past omissions, and if we continue to make omissions in the present the price tags will continue to inflate for the future.

The great reluctance of the ordinary citizen to pay for social and environmental costs expressed itself to governments as an unwillingness to pay additional taxes. Governments went along, and as much as they could, allowed cities to deteriorate and health problems to mount. But this compounded the costs, until they became so great, and affected so many, that government had to act. To avoid a conflict between the growing numbers who were now demanding necessary services and the rest who were refusing to pay for them governments discovered the deficit budget, and tried to borrow their way out. This government borrowing, and the tendency to pay for it with unwarranted new paper money, has become one of the prime inflation factors in industrial societies.

Risk-taking used to be part of the free market process. If the risk was worth it, the venture would be made. The greater the risk, the greater the rewards. It was this element of risk that justified the profit. The risks that private enterprise used to take are now expected to be borne by society, while private enterprise retains the profits. We see it in the building of nuclear plants that are not liable for the damages they might cause should something go wrong; we see it in the bailing out of large companies with taxpayers' money. The notion that business should be risk-free has gained so much acceptance that the largest business transaction in world history—the sale of $7 billion in uranium by Denison and Preston mines to Ontario Hydro—was conducted on a cost-plus basis. The mines were guaranteed a profit regardless of their costs. They no longer had to assume any risk. The risk was assumed by society. The cost of that risk is yet another contribution to inflation.

So are the growing number of transaction costs. Selling a house or running a small business used to be a simple matter. Now lawyers are virtually mandatory in both instances. Innumerable forms now need filing; not to protect the parties involved but to facilitate the collection of taxes. The average small businessman spends $5,000 per year filling out forms. The federal government, recognizing this problem, has organized a new government office whose only function is to reduce the amount of paperwork government requires. It's known as the bureaucracy's bureaucracy.

Lawyers now do much the same work as accountants, and both professions have been reduced to performing clerical functions by the vast array of government regulations. Governments and some business functions have outgrown human scale, complicating simple matters with inflationary sur-costs that do nothing to affect the final product or service in anything but cost.

Conserver principles could be used to simultaneously solve all the causes of inflation in our industrialized society. By definition, a conserver society strives to be sustainable and self-reliant. While recognizing the need for centralized systems in our society (such as the telephone system) a conserver society doesn't automatically recognize an advantage in systems being centralized. There is no advantage in depending on a power plant hundreds of miles away when power can be more dependably provided on your own property.

Removing the present bias toward large enterprises would see a shift to decentralized systems, a shift away from large bureaucracies and the costs they involve. This shift, accomplished through the conservation of capital, would also see a move toward smaller-scale technologies that would simplify and deflate current costs of doing business.

Decentralized systems don't depend on huge oil tankers that run aground leaving slicks behind that pollute coasts and destroy fisheries; they don't depend on massive tankers for liquefied natural gas, a substance so volatile that an explosion caused by a single spark would obliterate any evidence the tanker existed. Decentralized systems involve less risk. The risk can then be afforded by the risk-taker the way other risks are managed—through insurance companies. (Insurance companies find centralized systems such as nuclear installations and super tankers so risky they're uninsurable.)

Decentralized systems also require less capital; their cost is lower; diversity is encouraged. Having several smaller systems in place of one large one increases flexibility should one system break down.

In a conserver society social and environmental costs would not be sloughed off on other parts of society or onto future generations. They would be reflected directly in the cost of the product provided. Products tending to be socially or environmentally costly would have a higher overall cost, leading to less use or to innovations to reduce those costs. Instead of being hidden in someone else's ledger, where their sudden appearance becomes inflationary, social and environmental costs, as constant or decreasing factors, would no longer be inflationary.

The price of our resources would not continually climb. A conserver society running on renewable energy and using recycled materials would not be continually confronting shortages. Once the systems were in place, the sources of supplies would be known. Costs would tend to go down as improved technologies increased the efficiency of our use of energy and streamlined the recycling process. Products would be pre-designed with recycling in mind. Producing more durable products would stretch our material supplies as would the effect of synergy—doing more with less. Whatever need we'd have for more expensive, mined materials would be slowed to such a rate that the increasing costs of extraction and refining would be negligible and totally offset by the savings in recycling.

Setting the recycling system in place would involve an initial start-up expense; not continuous inflationary rises. This one-time expenditure would virtually guarantee that costs would not increase thereafter. With costs once again under control, the concerns of traditional economics become anachronistic. Prices rise when there is great demand for products. This demand can't be met by traditional economies because the demand is artifically created—there will always be more demand than supply. But in a conserver society the role of advertising will change from one of creating wants to one of providing information. With demand no longer tied to production, demand can now be met.

Lowering demand by taking money out of circulation doesn't work in our industrial society. Because large corporations and industries are outside the control of the free market, they don't respond to either fiscal or monetary policy. They are able to raise prices (because they haven't previously maximized profits) despite the attempt of government to lower them. They would not escape so easily in a conserver society. With centralized control no longer favoured the role of industrial giants would diminish, forcing them to maximize profits and respond to the forces of the market place, and government policy.

Once profits are maximized, unions would also lose much of

their bargaining power. Since companies would have already raised prices to the point they're maximizing profits (from which unions would have already won their wage gains) there would be less for unions to bargain for, and more resistance from companies if they tried. The wage-price spiral would be harder to set in motion. Since the elimination of planned obsolescence and the use of more durable products would increase real wealth by reducing real costs, unions would not be under pressure to raise wages. But raises would nevertheless come. A conserver society would become progressively more efficient, allowing non-inflationary raises to come from rising productivity.

18 The Materialization of Jobs

JOBS, LIKE EVERYTHING else, cost money.

To create one job in our resource industries requires an investment of $100,000 or more. If the job involves extracting minerals from our far north, an investment of over $1 million per job can be required. The money isn't spent to produce the job; it's spent to produce the profits, which everyone concedes are good for society. The fact that a job is created along the way is just further proof of the social value the mining operation has—something the industry can point to with pride whenever it seeks further tax breaks from governments.

But if jobs are a measure of social value, the manufacturing industries are the prime do-gooders. It only takes $25,000 to produce a job here: money invested in manufacturing makes 40 times more of an impact on job creation than equal sums spent searching for oil in the Arctic. Knowing this, wise politicians have tried to develop manufacturing industries in Canada. Thinking our domestic market too small to support most manufacturing industries, they've also usually tried to help our manufacturers sell to other countries.

Yet, despite their best attempts, manufacturing's share of our exports has been steadily declining for more than a decade. Our exports, as a percentage of production, are smaller than Portugal's, Spain's, Yugoslavia's, Ireland's or Mexico's. Canada now imports 50% more finished goods than in 1966, more goods than any other self-respecting nation. These imports are responsible for our single largest trade deficit—a staggering $11 billion a year in finished goods. That $11 billion a year is generously creating a lot of jobs for our trading partners. It could be thought of as our main contribution to foreign aid— usually aid to countries more affluent than ours. The jobs that Canada creates abroad are being created at the expense of Canadian jobs at home.

Research and development is important to a country's manufacturing capability. As countries become more highly developed, they're expected to increase their imports of low-technology goods produced by less sophisticated countries having lowlier labour rates. In theory, these extra imports result when a country gets smart and its low technology capabilities shift to high technology manufacturing.

Canada has been confounding the theorists. At the same time we are increasing our imports of low technology goods, in equal proportions we are increasing our imports of high technology goods. Conventional economists know that the combination of research and manufacturing equals jobs. Government sources estimate that, if Canada had Sweden's innovative and entrepreneurial skills, there would be about 35,000 more scientists and engineers in the industrial sector and between 2 and 4 million more jobs.

But our innovative skills are in decline. Canada ranks an embarassing fourteenth in research and development among OECD nations, just ahead of Greece and Turkey. The Swiss outperform us six to one. Our entrepreneurial skills fare even worse.

It isn't as if we haven't tried. For decades, our governments have embarked on scores of concerted programs. The result has been coordinated confusion. After World War II, Canada, in full economic development, could see it was unable to meet its needs for highly qualified manpower. The doors were opened to immigrants, who did their best to bail us out. By 1961, postwar immigrants had filled one quarter of our professional positions.

Faced with continuing shortages, federal and provincial governments undertook a deliberate policy of expanding higher education. By the 1960s university enrolment had tripled to 350,000 and another 150,000 students were squeezed into newly created community colleges. Meanwhile, to provide teachers with advanced degrees to advance these students to degrees, Canadian universities began shaping their curricula to produce highly qualified teachers, research supervisors, and professors. In the process they forgot to educate highly qualified people for government and business. Although the general level of education was raised, this oversight led to our managerial positions being filled by relative incompetents. Man for man, Canadian workers out-produce American workers while Canadian managers are outdone by their American counterparts.

And, to add to the confusion, now that the baby-boom children have all grown up, Canada has far more teachers than it knows how to use.

Raising the education level has a direct effect on raising the productivity of workers. Ontario, with the best-educated labour force, also has the highest productivity. Next come Alberta, British Columbia, Saskatchewan, and Quebec, whose productivity is well below the national average. Quebec's is low because its labour and management are less educated, having the highest proportion of workers who haven't gone beyond elementary school.

Attempts by governments to make manufacturing viable by improving our innovative ability have all fallen to pieces. Education outlays are being cut back. Innovation has all but stopped. Tax advantages for research and development have done little or no good. Though sizeable efforts, they've been based on piecemeal policies, compromised from the start through lack of comprehensive planning.

While these government steps may have given manufacturing a push, the push had no direction. Canadian manufacturers, told to produce for world markets, didn't know where to start. Told to produce for Canadian markets, they found there were no standards to produce to. Foreign producers were at least on an equal footing on the Canadian manufacturer's home ground.

Conserver principles would provide the direction, would result in viable manufacturing industries. Setting efficiency standards based on Canadian needs would create a distinct Canadian market for Canadian manufacturers. Distinctively Canadian products would require distinctively Canadian research and development efforts, assuring our innovative abilities stay at home. Canada would at last develop a strong technological base. From this base we could develop exports to countries with similar needs to ours.

To raise the money to finance a manufacturing industry a conserver society would only have to look to itself. Reversing Canada's historic tendency to borrow increasingly abroad, conservation of capital at home would save us $20 billion a year at only a 10% overall efficiency improvement. These savings would be available for investment.

Invested in our traditional resource industries, say in bold energy projects in the Arctic, where $1 million in investment is required per job produced, the $20 billion would yield 20,000 jobs. Subtracted from Canada's approximately 1 million unemployed that would leave us with approximately 980,000 jobless, a reduction in our unemployment rate of 0.2%. It would not do very much.

Invested in less remote resource regions, where a $100,000 investment produces a job, the $20 billion would yield 200,000 jobs. That would lower our unemployment level to 800,000, still somewhat less than laudable. Invested in manufacturing industries, where $25,000 produces a job, the $20 billion saved by a conserver society would produce 800,000 jobs, lowering our level of unemployment to 200,000, or about 2%. For a conventional economy, this would create an altogether different problem. Full employment is considered 3%-3.5% unemployment. A 2% rate of unemployment would be considered too low to maintain a fluid labour pool: industry would have difficulty finding workers on short notice. We would have an over-employment problem on our consciences.

Concepts of employment will have to be rethought. The job-creation potential of a conserver society is so great that jobs would become as plentiful as we permit. Having the capacity to manufacture our own goods would mean, in addition to the annual amount saved through conservation, an annual amount not spent on imports. That amount, spent in Canada, would produce more jobs, producing more goods. As we would develop more export markets for these goods, the job creation potential would expand further.

Our concerns would shift from how to find jobs for our workers to how to find workers to fill our jobs. Emphasis would be placed on how to get the most out of workers. The adoption of a conserver society would mark the beginning of a search to match appropriate workers to appropriate jobs, and the beginning of a new work ethic.

Getting more out of the labour force will require further upgrading education facilities. Five million Canadians are functionally illiterate and virtually unemployable in an advanced society. Of the 5 million, one million have less than a grade 5 education, and 3.2 million live in urban areas where jobs often require more sophistication. In areas such as Newfoundland, fully half the adult population has less than a grade 9 education.

Even universities are now finding that large proportions of their applicants are functionally illiterate and require remedial reading lessons before becoming worthy of a college degree.

The present glut of teachers, if employed to wipe out this illiteracy, could be turned to advantage through adult-education programs and better child-education. We could solve the problem of adult illiteracy before it starts. Just reducing the number of children per classroom from 30 or more to 20 would provide 50% more teaching jobs while giving our future workers the extra attention in education they require.

Canada has often been caught short of skilled workers of all descriptions, even in times of soaring unemployment. Industry's solution was to recruit skilled workers abroad. This did little to ease unemployment at home. Apprenticeship programs, historically run by industry to prevent bottlenecks in labour supply, have become the responsibility of governments not up to the task. Canada Manpower, formed for the purpose of coordinating the needs of business with the needs of labour, maintains its remarkable record of displeasing more employers and employees alike than any other government department (with the possible exception of the tax department). Surprisingly, the only government agency that has played a significant part in maintaining job skills has been the Unemployment Insurance Commission. By providing the unemployed with enough time to find work in their own field, the skills of the work force have not become eroded.

A conserver economy, though producing many jobs, would also produce some dislocations. Outdated skills would require updating. Needed skills would need to be safeguarded. With pressure off Manpower to push unqualified workers into jobs they aren't trained for, and pressure off the UIC to push legitimate claimants off the benefit rolls, these agencies could concentrate on fulfilling their original mandates. Manpower could make retraining its mission while unemployment benefits could be strengthened to give skilled workers the opportunity to put their skills to work.

Many of the jobs produced by a conserver society would go to meeting the private needs of its citizens. Many would go toward meeting public needs. With capital and labour freed for the public purpose, we would note an apparent paradox of the conserver society: money spent for public goods and services would save on overall costs of goods and services.

Jobs in public transit would save public funds in building and maintaining roads while saving energy and making car travel more enjoyable for those who don't appreciate the luxuries of rush hour. Jobs in health care that result in a healthier populace would save costs in future medical bills, lost income to the workers, and lost productivity to their employers. Jobs in education would lead to a better, more successful workforce, more likely to meet the aspirations of its members while expanding their personal horizons. Jobs in our judicial system would save the costs of interminable delays to business projects unable to act, often for years, while matters wait to be heard before the court.

And all these jobs would save communities the costs of

welfare and their citizens many of the personal tragedies associated with joblessness: personal degradation and the loss of self-respect; impoverishment and the rise of family tensions; humiliation and the feeling of aimlessness.

19 *Reworking the Work Ethic*

ONE OF CANADA'S labour leaders likes to tell the story of John Kennedy's fear (as candidate for the U.S. presidency) of being accused of never having worked a day in his life. The day of reckoning came at a factory gate, where JFK stood shaking hands of workers leaving at the end of their afternoon shift.

"I hear you never worked a day of your life," one oldtimer said. "Is it true?"

The future president braced himself and admitted it was.

"Son, I've been working here for more than 40 years, and let me tell you," the oldtimer spat. "You ain't missed a thing."

There is no joy in work for work's sake. Though the devil may find work for idle hands, there is little that's godly in employing those hands to paste labels on deodorant bottles, rinse dishes in a greasy spoon, or scribble out telephone orders the morning after the annual sale on toilet items is announced.

Yet a job, any job, is widely perceived as having a social purpose. The young mother who drops her child off at a day-care en route to duties at an office typing pool may do so less for the money than for the desire to express herself in a meaningful way. The artist who gives up his garret, after years of struggling to become another Van Gogh, and turns his talents to decorating billboards will be greeted with satisfaction by all those relieved he's no longer wasting his time. The hobbyist who makes his private preoccupation a public occupation will suddenly be viewed with respect although all that may have changed is the location of his activities.

The better the job is paid, the higher the social purpose. Until he's replaced by his subordinate, the boss will always be judged the worthier of the two. In selecting a new employee for a job the candidate with the highest previous salary will be thought the most capable. The lower the salary, the lower the social worth. Being paid nothing implies no social worth. Unless very young, very old or very rich, everyone not gainfully employed can expect to be an object of scorn. This is a normal manifestation of the modern work ethic, an ethic that continues to promote the traditional requirement of work long after the traditional requirement of work has disappeared.

Before the rise of industrialism it was not necessary to proclaim the virtues of the work ethic. For most people, work and survival went hand in hand. Those that worked hard had a reasonable expectation of survival. Those that didn't, died. The proponents of work had a convincing argument.

People unable to work have always been expected to compensate for this deficiency. It's never been enough for a beggar to extend an open palm. Unless the gesture is accompanied by the sight of weeping sores, mutilated limbs, or, at the very least, the sound of piteous wails, few will call upon their humanitarian instincts and shunt money into that palm. To do so would be thought immoral.

Legislation promoting the work ethic retained the traditional morality. The Poor Laws, passed under Queen Elizabeth I in 1601, marked the first time a government formally recognized a responsibility to the unemployed. Work projects were funded to assure jobs for anyone wanting them. Of course, provisions in the law made clear that this work was relief and not prosperity. The projects involved menial tasks such as breaking stones and straightening roads at wages substantially lower than anywhere else in the country. When work projects couldn't be created, debt-ridden families were carted off to work houses. Here they pondered the work ethic as they waited for money or a job to pay off their debts.

Although work houses disappeared in the late nineteenth century, the attitude that created them lived on. As recently as the early 1900s it was the popular consensus that people were unemployed because they weren't willing to change their ways, not because there was an insufficiency of jobs. British legislation in 1905 insisted that government relief work, which paid a much lower wage than private industry, be awarded only to those "honestly desirous of finding work" and of "good character." This clause in the act eliminated five out of every six applicants. In one case, an individual applied for work-relief after his company went bankrupt. Although he'd worked for seven consecutive years at the same firm he was judged "incapable of holding down a job" and refused work-relief.

Even when work-relief was granted, it failed to solve the problem of unemployment. Although these jobs were snapped up whenever the government saw fit to distribute them, and the pay was so low that they perpetuated the workers in poverty, governments couldn't afford them. Cheap labour is not always economical, at least not in a society which has developed a specialized labour market. When unskilled workers are asked to do the work of the skilled, or when those skilled in one field are expected to be equally skilled in another, the results are usually more costly than if the going rate was paid for the properly trained personnel.

Job creation programs failed either to alleviate the condition of the unemployed or to provide economical labour for government projects. It was much cheaper, governments found, to simply give the unemployed money. Although fearful this would destroy the work ethic, governments saw no suitable alternatives.

This realization (already present by the turn of the century) saw the rise of social insurance legislation. Welfare programs and unemployment insurance schemes became commonplace, particularly in the northern European countries. Some of these countries, such as Sweden and Denmark, are now characterized as being welfare states. Others, such as Switzerland (the first country to experiment with an unemployment insurance system) and Germany (the first country to adopt a social insurance system) have among the most generous social benefits in the world. These are the very countries which also have the highest standards of living in the world, and the strongest adherence to the work ethic.

Offering workers security, whether through social insurance schemes or through generous wages, has only tended to reinforce the work ethic. Like anything else, work, when it's meaningful, reinforces itself. When the purpose of a job is individual survival, and the better the job done the better the prospects for survival, work is extraordinarily meaningful. It is indispensable to life.

When the purpose of a job is the work itself, when becoming a scientist or a sailor or a social worker is the end in itself, and doing the work well satisfies the soul, work is extraordinarily meaningful. It is indispensable to happiness. When the purpose of a job is to provide the means to acquire goods, and work is seen as a necessary evil to pay for the goods, the work itself stops being meaningful. The goods become indispensable to happiness, and when work can be avoided it is. Those at work tend to put in time and those out of work rely on society. The work ethic can't be eroded by making work more pleasant, or more remunerative, or more secure. It can only be eroded by making work less meaningful.

Overemphasis on money has changed the work ethic. The traditions of carrying on with the family farm, or following in a father's footsteps seem quaint to many young graduates having the opportunity for more remunerative careers. Even that most hallowed of professionals—the family physician—now thinks in terms of increasing his volume of business: controlling the hours in which his patients can become sick to eliminate the need for time-consuming housecalls, and hiring small numbers of nurses (to look after the preliminaries) to increase the daily droves of patients to whom he's able to give personal attention.

Along with pride in being a big money earner has come pride in working for big money earners—the large corporations. Employees often identify themselves more with their company than with their work: the work ethic has been transformed into the job ethic. Being at work, either for the money or for the prestige, has become more important than getting the work done well. This has been reinforced by the effects of automation, which de-emphasizes the luxury of craftsmanship and stresses the profits of mass production. An assembly-line worker finds it hard to get satisfaction from knowing four welds in a car are his. That information, conveyed to a friend, would not be likely to extract admiration. So it isn't, and the chief aspects of a man's activities—the work he does—stops being a source of pride. Solace must be sought elsewhere, and in the process, the quality of the work, and the work ethic, suffers.

The success of Northern European countries in resisting an erosion of the work ethic is only partly due to strong social insurance legislation. Having, for the most part, smaller-scale economies than the North American economy they have had less of a tendency to rely on mass production; and where their own multinationals have automated work they've had more of a tendency to accommodate automation to human needs.

Sweden's Volvo plants are a classic example. When they were re-assembled in the 1950s and 1960s to resemble North American auto plants workers rebelled at becoming cogs in Volvo's production machine. The discontent threatened to lower worker productivity, so Volvo reorganized one plant to respond to its workers needs. They arranged workers in teams, each with its own small workshop, and each accountable for one complete system in a car, such as the electrical system. The teams assigned work to their own members, and even determined their own working methods. Traditional engineering thinking said such a method couldn't be efficient, but motivated workers proved that thinking wrong. None of the conventional plants could outperform the reorganized plant.

For work to be meaningful the results of that work must be meaningful. As products become less meaningful, as more and more of our necessities are met and more and more of what we produce are luxuries, the importance of working for those luxuries diminishes. People work less.

In 1850 the average work week was about 70 hours. To keep hovel and home required working the equivalent of a six-day week, from 6:00 in the morning to 6:00 in the evening. A hundred years later life had become somewhat easier. To live in a style that would have impressed most of their forefathers took only a 40-hour week—the 1950 average. Moonlighting an extra 30 hours a week was possible but not plausible in an age when all necessities and some comforts were already being met. The extra work would not justify the extra rewards.

Labour leaders are now pressing for, and will soon get, a 30- or 32-hour work week. Although the rest of society may protest against the greed of unions in making these extravagant demands, once the demands are met society will see the injustice of not having a reduced work week as well. The 30-hour week will become our new average. Levels of production that could have been possible had the work week stayed at 40 hours will be foregone without a serious protest. Few will weep over products not yet conceived of and so not yet wanted.

And as goods continue to become relatively less consequential to us our work week will decline further. Jobs, by becoming more scarce, will become more highly prized—not as a means of acquiring goods because goods will have decreasing value, not to ensure survival because survival has long since stopped being a central problem, but in themselves, as their own rewards.

This will be the continuation of another historic trend.

Some jobs are more desirable than others. To most, being a secretary in a posh office building downtown beats being a secretary in a rundown building downtown. The posh job usually pays less. Similarly blue collar jobs, generally seen as less prestigious than their white collar counterparts, now tend to pay more. For someone to select teaching, or science, or journalism as a career means, in most cases, to pass up a higher salary as a garbageman, or carpenter, or construction worker.

Although certain professions—medicine and the legal profession in particular—have been able to keep their prices high this will be a short-lived phenomenon. The myth that somehow the ordeal of spending six or eight years in college entitles a person to greater rewards than someone who worked for those six or eight years, or the myth that the expense of tuition—when 85% of education costs are borne by society—justifies later recouping that expense with inflated fees, will be shortly disposed of. The large numbers of doctors and lawyers finding no work, and the forthcoming decisions to permit advertising in these presently closed-shop professional societies, will expose them to market forces. The large numbers of young doctors of the future will find themselves selecting medicine despite the lower incomes it will provide. They will do so because, like the doctors of old, medicine is their calling.

In a choice between two desirable jobs, most now would opt for the better paying one. In a choice between two jobs, one more desirable than the other, most would select the more desirable. Leaders in industry gladly take enormous pay cuts to join governments in prestige roles. The fact our prime minister earns less than the average hockey player provides him little incentive to don his hockey skates and try out for the big leagues.

In the 1850s, aside from a handful of educators, artists, clerics, and scientists, there were few who earned their income more from the workings of their mind than the sweat on their brow. Canada might have had a few hundred. Today the menial chores are performed by the minority, and the trend in this direction is accelerating. Workers in the service industries outnumber workers producing goods by a factor of two-to-one; 88% of all new jobs produced in the last five years have been in the service sector.

De-emphasizing the production of material goods will free enormous amounts of investment capital. Part of it could be used to compensate for the decision our society has taken to pay more for undesirable jobs. It could become increasingly profitable to replace monotonous or unrewarding work with machines. But the largest shift will be toward ever-increasing investments in human capital, primarily education, to provide entry for people into the types of work most meaningful to them.

Those in desirable professions—and their offspring—rarely leave them. The child of a chemist or an accountant would be looked upon with horror if he chose to become a factory worker. If ill equipped to become a professional, he nevertheless stays in the fringes of the professional class—as an investment dealer or a salesman.

Those not of the professional class often aspire to it, often push their children into careers they themselves were denied. That the trend in work has been away from the menial, toward the more mentally stimulating fields comes as no surprise.

Investment in human capital will lead to more people doing the kind of work they choose to—it will lead to a reinforcement of the work ethic.

The emphasis will turn to diverse intellectual interests—scientific, literary, cultural, artistic, and social concerns. Quality will predominate over quantity, one new Van Gogh seen to be worth an infinite number of billboard artists in a world no longer preoccupied with selling the item on that billboard.

Methods of work will become as diverse as the purposes of work. With jobs becoming secondary to the work that needs to be done, the over-regimented, under-utilized structures of jobs will break down. The Monday-to-Friday phenomenon is already giving way to four- and three-day weeks; the 9:00-5:00 habit to workdays that begin at 6:00 or 7:00 and end at 3:00 or 4:00.

Innovative work options have barely begun to be practised. Sharing the same job between two people is still a rare occurrence, mainly limited to a very few husband and wife teams interested in differently sharing their home and work responsibilities. Yet there would be many advantages in work sharing for other people, for other ends. Executives who like to golf mornings can share jobs with executives who like to sail afternoons. Those who like to travel winters can share jobs with those who like to travel summers. Work-exchange programs could allow workers at plants in Halifax to switch for weeks at a time with workers at plants in Vancouver.

Increasing worker options would be rewarding for employers as well, in higher morale and higher productivity. Many jobs lend themselves to more than one skill, and could bring highly specialized talents together at a normal wage. Great savings are also possible by redesigning offices for round-the-clock operation, saving rent and office equipment. Not everyone likes to work the midnight hours but many would prefer nothing better. When jobs don't require getting in touch with clients—as many jobs do—there's no reason why a salesman's office by day couldn't be converted to a bookkeeper's office by night.

Too often, we forget why we work. It is to eliminate deprivation and further our spiritual well-being. We work to be happy. Blind adherence to the shell of the old work ethic, which distortedly demands work, any work, even forced work as a social good is an attachment to another form of slavery.

The old work ethic is the antithesis of a work ethic in a freed society, a freed society appreciative of the real work that lies ahead.

PART FIVE

Introducing the Conserver Society

20 *Who Has to Do What*

A CONSERVER SOCIETY is a self-fulfilling goal—we can achieve it as quickly or as slowly as we choose. We have the technology —much of it has been around longer than we have. We have the experience—we need to man no more demonstration models to prove over and over again that the sun can keep us warm. We have the need—Canada's economic and social well-being will otherwise remain forever insecure.

What we need is the will.

A century ago our nation was in the midst of building a trans-continental railroad. Now known as our "national dream," it was then thought of as a national nightmare, confronted by natural obstacles of magnitudes thought by many to be insuperable. Despite the natural obstacles—and unnatural ones such as political confusion, and wholesale graft—the building of the CPR had become a national priority. Those who said it would never be built found themselves paying homage to it a few short years later.

A decade ago a man stepped on the surface of the moon. In many third world countries, this event is still not believed by the general populace. Their sentiment was shared by Americans a decade before the space mission, when John Fitzgerald Kennedy announced that within 10 years the United States would be landing a man on the moon. At the time the idea seemed preposterous. With the technology still to be developed, with the resources still to be gathered, the general populace thought Kennedy naïve to think so much could be accomplished in so little time. Yet it also believed that supremacy in space was worthy of the nation's commitment. The goal was met in less than the time predicted.

A conserver society can be ours in less time than it took to drive that last spike of the railway, less time than it took to put a man on the moon. We have the option to create a society that has conserver values, that runs on renewable energy, that recycles all its materials, that is wholly sustainable and regenerative. In a five-to-ten year period most aspects of a conserver society could be phased in, most unwanted aspects of our presently unsustainable society could be phased out. Within a decade we could be visibly seen as a conserving state.

A conserver society is a conceptual force, it's not the final form for society. It opens up options in order to keep them open, not to fix our destiny to one narrow vision or another. Flexible, it can be achieved through many means; once in place, it can be made to respond to many needs. It prescribes nothing but a framework from which infinite combinations can interact and not self-destruct. A conserver society transcends traditional ideology. It's possible to have a communist conserver society as well as a capitalist conserver society. A conserver society can operate under a dictatorship or under a democracy. A strong dictator would have little trouble imposing his brand—he would have his society by fiat.

To get ours, in a democracy, requires the active cooperation of the members of society. There is no one course which must be followed but there is a direction toward goals that must be followed: the direction is toward the sustainable and away from the unsustainable; toward the self-sufficiency of individuals and away from the control of institutions; toward the actively involved; toward a balance in our biosphere. The recommendations which follow provide one set of many possible sets of options.

What Government Has to Do

The role of any modern government with integrity is to try to eliminate itself. Karl Marx expected his communist state to "wither away" as its citizens achieved total liberty. Anarchists want decentralized, small-scale communities that govern themselves. Capitalists incline towards *laissez-faire* policies (except when it affects them personally) in the philosophical belief that the state has no necessary function. The founding fathers of America felt even standing armies were a threat to individual freedoms. In this they showed solidarity with the beliefs of Karl Marx, and the actions of anarchists. But until governments can achieve for society a level of well-being so great that people will despise them sufficiently to relinquish them, governments are seen as necessary evils.

By this standard, the government of a conserver society will have its share of evil—but it will be a smaller share. It will practice what it preaches, but it will preach too. Governments preach through legislation.

Adopt Total-Costing of Products

The cost of a product should reflect all the costs associated with it, including costs that occur after the product is sold, such as the costs of pollution and the costs of disposal. Often, the future costs are difficult to calculate, or represent a risk which might not materialize (e.g. potential damage from a nuclear reactor). As with many other risk-taking events, the manufacturer should be required to take out insurance against the event's occurence. Risks that are too great to be insurable indicate the benefits of a product do not outweigh its short-comings. Adoption of total-costing would lead to the design of products that pollute less and are easy to recycle, since their costs would be lower than high-polluting and hard-to-recycle products.

Introduce Mandatory Life-Cycle Costing

When a consumer makes any purchase, he should know its future costs as well as initial price. This involves disclosure by the producer, where applicable, of how long the good or service will last, how much it will cost for servicing or repair in that period, what average fuel costs will be, and any other relevant information. Costs should include total-costing and be based on Canadian factors (for example, because of climate the durability of a car will be different in Manitoba than Mississippi).

Accuracy of the life-cycle estimates can be insured by private insurers. The government need not set up a regulatory agency to check manufacturers' data. Private individuals and public interest groups would be well-disposed toward reporting violations and taking remedial action. This legislation would achieve two broad objectives: provide information to help purchasers make efficient choices and create a distinctive Canadian market for Canadian manufacturers.

Encourage Research and Development in Industry
With a Canadian market created, Canadian technology will have a reason to stay in Canada. The present 5% tax credit for research and development should be raised to 25% for industry. As many significant innovations are the result of private efforts, a similar credit should be available to individual inventors. Government research efforts should shift away from questionable projects, such as nuclear development, and focus more on growth industries such as the renewable energy field. Wherever possible, government research and development should be contracted out to the private sector. The national expenditure for research and development in Canada should be raised from the present 1% to 3% of GNP.

Remove Bias in Favour of Capital-Intensive Projects
Large, capital-intensive projects have their place in our society but not at the expense of smaller-scale ventures. To bring about a better balance in how capital is allocated, interest rates should increase as the size of loans increase. Also, existing legislation, by favouring our primary resource industries with reduced freight rates and capital-depletion allowances, actively

discourages the recycling industry as well as low-capital (i.e. labour-intensive) projects. Biased legislation of this nature should be phased out.

Promote Efficient and Durable Products
Wasteful buying practices hurt more than the purchaser—they hurt society. To compensate and promote the conservation of capital, inefficient goods and services should be surtaxed on the basis of their efficiency. The most efficient purchase would have no surtax, the least-efficient purchase the greatest surtax. This tax should be levied at the manufacturing stage, as federal sales tax is, to avoid complicating the normal procedure of making a purchase.

Bring Advertising Under Existing Business Practice Guidelines
For advertising to provide a legitimate business function, it must be informative. Non-informative advertising should not be considered a legitimate business expense for tax purposes, as it presently is. Advertising that is ideological in nature, such as lifestyle advertising, should be subject to the same rules governing advertising of political philosophies. Advocacy advertising, allowing equal time for views counter to those advertised, should become standard, as a principle of fair play. Half the time any advertiser allocates to the promotion of any product or goal, whether it be consistent with a conserver society or not, should be made available to a public interest group or institution having an opposing perspective.

Consider Foreign Ads Taxable Gifts
American-owned businesses operating in Canada (branch-plant operations) often benefit from advertising by the parent company on the U.S. television networks. This increased exposure for the branch plants gives them an unfair advantage over Canadian-owned businesses promoting similar products. To equalize this free benefit the branch-plant operations receive, these ads, when beamed into Canada, should be considered a taxable gift by the head office to the Canadian subsidiary.

Transform Our Garbage Collection System into a 100%
Recycling System
Garbage now has great value when recycled into heat energy.

As it begins to pay manufacturers to design with recycling in mind, the value of garbage—both as energy and as scrap material—will increase, justifying ever-increasing recycling technologies to salvage more and more of what we throw out. A computerized accounting system will eventually be needed to credit those who throw out garbage for its value.

Test All New Chemicals Before Commercialization
As a matter of morality and economic sense, new chemicals should not be permitted to be used commercially until their effects on our health and environment have been thoroughly tested. Canada should promote international testing standards be adopted to facilitate greater cooperation among countries in sharing this burden.

Guarantee Sun Rights
With total costing of non-renewable forms of energy enforced, solar energy (and other renewable forms) will become a striking bargain. But unless access to the sun is guaranteed, homes using solar collectors could find their energy supply curtailed should an apartment building be built next door. Sun rights were once considered a normal property right in Canada. They should be brought back.

Make Public Utilities More Responsive to the Public
Electric rates should be based on the costs of producing additional amounts of electricity to best let those who use less pay less. Individual metering of apartments will also promote thrift. When an individual finds that he can improve his fuel bill by insulating or implementing other conservation measures, his utility should be required to loan him the money to do it, and be repaid from the individual's fuel savings with interest. Individuals and industries that generate their own electricity should be allowed to hook into the energy grid and sell their excess electricity to the utilities.

Remove Disincentives to Conserve
Local by-laws, and the raising of tax assessments, discourage many homeowners from investing in energy-saving improvements such as solar heating or insulation. Governments should refrain from reassessing the value of a conservation-improved home. Also, car and van pools are presently inhibited through insurance restrictions, inability to collect fees, and income tax penalties. Governments should treat car and van pools as a transportation system.

Practice What It Preaches
Government at all levels, spending over $40 billion per annum, represents Canada's largest consumer. This vast purchasing power should be used to encourage business and industry to produce with conservation in mind. Governments should specify insulation standards when renting office space, buy products on the basis of their life-cycle costs and favour Canadian-owned firms when purchasing any good or service.

Eliminate Red Tape by Simplifying Bureaucratic Requirements
Taxing and other policies have become more and more complex in sophisticated attempts to remove inequities. The result has been to become inequitable through severely straining the resources of those taxed. Small businessmen, for example, estimate unnecessary paperwork costs them an average of $5,000 per year.

Upgrade Existing Legislation to Aid Dislocated Workers
Unemployment insurance programs exist to aid the many workers who are out of a job. Manpower retraining programs exist for increasing numbers of workers with outdated skills. Travel grants and moving grants exist for those needing to search for work in other parts of the country.

During the transition to a conserver society, as we switch from an economy based on non-renewable resources to one based on recycling, an increased number of workers could be temporarily caught between jobs, needing to be taught new skills or moved to new locations. Yet the existing aids to workers are often meager by international standards, and largely unknown to many of those who could use them most.

Existing legislation should be strengthened and publicized to aid workers in the transition.

Eliminate the Minimum Wage and Social Welfare Programs
The pricing mechanism of the free market is greatly distorted by the myriad of social welfare plans, and the minimum wage, which prevent people from working for nothing—if they choose—and companies from obtaining cheap labour where they can. The minimum wage has had questionable social value in Canada, since it is so low it only perpetuates the worker in poverty. (Where the minimum wage is high, as Denmark's minimum of $11,000, for example, it has helped make the country one of the wealthiest per capita in the world.)

To replace the duplication of these social payments, and the government bureaucracies that run them, a universal negative income tax system should be adopted, guaranteeing no family unit lives below the poverty line. A family that earned less than the poverty line would receive a negative income tax to bring it to the poverty line. A flat income tax rate of 50% could then be applied to all family income above the poverty line, with no exemptions necessary.

A taxation method such as this would simplify tax calculations, assure that no one lived in poverty, eliminate the need for several huge government bureaucracies, and permit workers to select jobs most appropriate for themselves at salaries agreeable to business. There would be no inequity if, for example, a company made working conditions so attractive all working members of a family decided to work for nothing. Their total income would be the same as if they didn't work at all, and the business would benefit from cheap labour. If the company wasn't able to attract cheap labour, it would have the choice of paying more than the poverty line (in which case normal market forces would determine the salary) or replacing the workers with machines.

The limit to which any individual or family could exploit the system would be to the extent of the poverty line—hardly much of an incentive and about the same as present welfare schemes. The only policing that would be needed would be to ensure family units didn't pretend to be living as individuals in order to claim marginally higher negative income taxes (the poverty line for a couple is less than twice the poverty lines of two individuals).

What Business and Industry Have to Do

Once Canadian industry has been freed from many of the restraints of government, once there is a distinct Canadian market to produce for and more of a free market environment to produce in, the challenge will be for business and industry to make our economy work. Opportunities in a conserver society will be unlimited and there will be responsibilities to accompany each one.

Launch a Design Revolution

Products designed to be durable, to use less materials, to be easily repaired, to pollute less, and have lower operating costs will suddenly be recognized for their value—their life-cycle costs will be lower than competing, less efficient brands. Design possibilities include the use of corrosion-resistant materials, replacement of rubber belts with gears, the sealing of sensitive parts, modular construction for easy repair, and updating and synergetic (doing more with less) innovations. Components made of different materials should be distinguishable and separable for scrapping, or they should form a useable mixture or alloy when scrapped together. Surface coatings should be designed not to create problems in recycling.

Set Industry-wide Efficiency Standards

Industry associations, in cooperation with public consumer groups, should agree on objective criteria for measurement of efficiency standards for goods and services. Monitoring how well products live up to their claims can remain a function of individuals and consumer groups.

Embark On an Intensive Research and Development Effort
The opportunities that exist lie mainly in conserver technologies yet to be discovered; the renewable energy, recycling, and pollution-abatement fields are all in their infancy. Electronics, the technology that best does more with less, should also have high priority. All research and development should be especially mindful of Canadian needs and the Canadian environment.

Develop a Used Appliance Market
The used car market recycles most cars manufactured, and over 50% of television sets are restored to use. Yet for most other appliances the used market is virtually non-existent. Only 3% of dishwashers survive a trade-in, for example.

Shift from Primary to Secondary Resource (Recycling) Industries
Dependence on our in-ground natural resources will be phased down as recycling technologies gain precedence. Most recycling that takes place is currently done by primary producers, whose expertise should be developed further by accelerating the movement toward more recycling.

Decentralize Big Business
Large organizations are finding diseconomies of scale when head offices must make decisions for branch plants thousands of miles away. Local resources tend not to be used to advantage, and head office overheads weigh down corporate superstructures when functions—such as accounting—are needlessly located at corporate headquarters. The communications industry has become so sophisticated, with information able to be relayed efficiently and instantaneously, that the best information can be available, and the decision-making process occur, locally.

Diversify
There is stability in diversity. Corporations will need to be increasingly flexible in a conserver society marked by rapid technological change. To avoid vested interests in outdated

enterprises, large corporations should diversify into varied fields to protect their shareholders and keep their managements intact.

Compete on the Basis of Price and Quality
The advertising industry should abandon non-informative advertising and develop industry criteria, with the cooperation of public interest groups, to define informative advertising. Consultation with groups in advance of broadcasting or publishing ads would often eliminate the need for advocacy advertising, and speed up the production process when advertising time or space needs to be shared with an opposing point of view.

Pay Their Own Way
When it is difficult to assume future risks, industries should seek insurance against them. Workman's Compensation Board premiums should be encouraged to pay for all occupational diseases.

Buy Canadian
Until foreign branch-plant operations produce for Canadian needs, companies wishing to promote the Canadian economy should favour Canadian-controlled enterprises.

Smooth Peak Loads
Staggered hours for employees, replacing business travel with conference calls, and helping to organize car pools will reduce the strain on existing systems while increasing efficiency and social options.

Re-establish Apprenticeship Programs
These can be run through engineering schools and community colleges or developed at industry locations. Without industry taking the initiative in ensuring the labour force is trained in skills that industry will require, industry will have to depend on time lags involved with Manpower retraining programs or on foreign labour.

What Individuals Have to Do

Individuals need not wait for events to unfold around them—in a democracy we have the responsibility to act as the catalyst to bring about necessary changes. It is this responsibility that forms the essence of a conserver society: we must take responsibility for our own actions. We must think about what we are doing, and whether we can do them better; about the systems we depend on and whether we want to continue to depend on them; about our relation to our surroundings and whether our gains in one area aren't made at an equal or greater loss in another.

There is little point ennumerating the course of action a conserver society demands from its citizens. It is diversity that characterizes the self-sustainability of a conserver society, and once we unleash our individual energies and begin to react to each other, to our biosphere, in conserver ways the limitless potential of our innovative capacity will begin to unfold.

This diversity is synergetic, it is unpredictable. In the recent past it has manifested itself in geodesic domes, food co-ops, new technologies such as solar power, organic farming, the updating of old technologies (such as windmills) into new, the environmental movement, and consumer groups. In the future it can be anything imaginable or unimaginable within the confines of the conserver ethic—it can be anything that keeps our world self-sustaining and regenerative.

21 *Who Gets Hurt in the Transition?*

NO ONE ARGUED more passionately or more persuasively for the benefits of the fluorocarbon spray can than Robert Abplanalp, its inventor and manufacturer, and the person who stood to lose most by its demise. Although environmentalists claimed that the fluorocarbons emitted during spraying could result in a rash of skin cancers by destroying the atmosphere's ozone layer, Abplanalp for years was able to refute the findings of some of the world's most eminent scientists. Finally, the weight of scientific evidence became so overwhelming the U.S. Food and Drug Administration could dawdle no longer: it announced that the fluorocarbon spray can would be banned. The very next day, Robert Abplanalp was pleased to announce the introduction of a new spray can which not only did away with the feared fluorocarbons but also outperformed the old spray can.

Such is the glory of the free enterprise system, and its genius. It has survived two world wars, outlasted scores of governments and political philosophies, and defied all attempts at economic regulation. While the number of democracies in the world declines, the number of free-enterprise systems increases. Dictatorships of the right aren't alone in preferring them. The Russians themselves have legalized the free market for non-military commodities. Left-wing dictatorships that still frown upon free markets generally have one anyway. Known as black markets, they co-exist quite happily, quite prosperously, and quite illegally along with state economies, and have been doing so as long as man has been trying to regulate man.

It is to the credit of Canadian bankers that, in the same breath that they demand less government intervention in banking, they can insist the federal government stop trust companies from expanding the banking services they provide. It is to the credit of our American-owned automobile industry that it lobbies against allowing European and Japanese cars into Canada on the grounds that the Canadian industry must be protected from foreign domination. The ground rules for business are constantly changing, and business has done no more than adapt to changing conditions; in doing so business has displayed extraordinary resiliency and innovation. It's hard to keep a good business down.

Poor businesses, those without the ability to adapt, fail as soon as they're put to the test. There were many personal tragedies when the horseless carriage began replacing the horse and buggy. Saddlemakers were thrown out of their jobs. Horseshoe manufacturers faced declining sales. Makers of horse-drawn carriages went under. (Great dramas are being played out today. The tobacco companies' virtual stampede in search of alternative products following the U.S. Surgeon General's report on the hazards of smoking is yet to see the final curtain, and we have barely begun the first act in seeing how manufacturers of baby foods and disposable diapers will respond to the plummeting birth rate.)

The tragedies took place not because the car had arrived but because the horse and buggy trade refused to believe the car could supplant the carriage. Those carriage makers who understood the industry would never be the same—people such as Fisher (of body-by-Fisher fame)—became the leaders in the new industry.

In retrospect, business does not look at the transition era around the turn of the century, when the car, plane, and electric lights were introduced, with sadness for the industries which were outmoded. That era is viewed as a triumph for industry, not a tragedy.

The horse and buggy business gave birth to the biggest business in the world. In Canada, Ford and General Motors are the largest companies year in, year out, with combined sales of $10 billion. They've held these positions because, for the better part of this century, they've created, led, or adapted to society's needs. They'll continue to hold their positions only as long as they continue to do so.

In the coming transition to a conserver society, there will be numerous business failures, numerous industries that will atrophy if they don't adapt. The changes on the face of society could be as fundamental as the changes accompanying industrialization. Their scope will be synergetic and impossible to predict.

Predictable, though, is who will get hurt. It will be those not up to the times, those unable to adapt. Anticipating the need for flexibility, the need to be able to respond to changing markets or even loss of entire markets, industry has already built up a widespread capability to adapt, a capability designed to let it capitalize on the consequences of change.

The 3M Company, long-known exclusively as makers of masking tape and Scotch tape, has branched out into no less than ten major product lines. Building on a team of market specialists (as opposed to a team of product managers), 3M products now surface in hardware and houseware departments, in sporting goods and stationery stores, in pharmacies and phonograph shops. The company produces scouring pads and fly fishing lines, timed-release plant food and cold-weather masks. The company produces innovation—3M will not be hurt in the transition to a conserver society. Innovation is a commodity that can prosper anywhere.

Molson's Brewery is another company that has developed a survival capability. Faced with declining earnings in the beer business, the company entered the do-it-yourself home improvement market by opening up a chain of Beaver Lumber retail outlets. Within two years Molson was registering an annual growth rate of 30%, with retail merchandise, thanks to Beaver Lumber, accounting for 28% of total company sales.

The do-it-yourself market was not Molson's first attempt at

diversification. Earlier attempts proved dismal failures, even when prospects seemed good. They failed because Molson's tried to diversify into unrelated fields, where it was out of its marketing depth. Molson's didn't recognize its strength lay with its strong, consumer-oriented management team.

Matching appropriate skills to appropriate challenges allows a brewery to tackle the apparently unrelated home improvement market, allows a cosmetics firm with a highly efficient door-to-door sales force to diversify into jewelry, allows a company with technical expertise in construction to diversify into farm machinery.

In future, it will allow manufacturers of private transit vehicles (automobiles) to diversify into public transit, primary resource industries to diversify into secondary (recycling) industries, and polluting companies to diversify into anti-pollution equipment. As is often the case, discoveries in one field will be useful to others. A large Canadian paper company, for example, faced with the costly disposal of waste pulp liquor, solved the problem by developing a process to extract from the liquor a chemical compound that's commonly used in the food and pharmaceutical industries. Today it dominates the market for this chemical and several of its derivatives.

Companies are often too quick to criticize government requirements they clean up their pollution, too pessimistic about the effects on their competitive position. The multi-national GAF corporation decided to throw in the towel in 1975 rather than comply with a government order to spend $3 million on pollution-control equipment for its Lowell, Vermont, asbestos mine. Mine workers, more optimistic and fearing for their jobs, bought GAF out at its market value of $50 per share and installed the equipment. Three years later, their average hourly wages had jumped from $3.26 to $4.96 and each $50 share was now worth $2,103. Having made their point, and their profits, the mine workers voted to sell out to private interests and leave the managing to others.

In Canada, there is yet to be found a single instance of pollution-control requirements turning a competitive industry into a non-competitive one. Affected industries complain, as they should in fulfilling their role, but when they are finally forced to comply they find the task is easier done than said.

Specific legislation in a conserver society will affect specific classes of industry. Efficiency standards based on Canadian needs will hurt all those companies selling us unsuitable products. For many foreign-owned manufacturers, staying in the Canadian market will stop being profitable. Other foreign-controlled corporations will exploit the new opportunities in Canada and find they're profitable for themselves and for the country.

Efficiency standards will only affect companies that have competition with superior standards. If they close, the more efficient firms can expand production to meet consumer demands. There will be no shortage of goods and services, only a shortage of inefficient goods and services.

A conserver society will stop favouring the large, capital-intensive industries at the expense of smaller ventures that have trouble getting their share of capital. Statistics Canada reports there are 206,695 enterprises in Canada. The top 500, which represents less than a quarter of one percent, account for 59.2% of the assets, 63.4% of the profits and 65.4% of the equity. The other 206,195 companies are left to divvy up the rest. With the bias toward the large industries removed, companies in the top 500 will tend to find excess capital no longer inexpensive, the companies in the bottom 200,000—the bottom 99.75%—will tend to find capital more accessible.

An industry directly affected by the transition to a conserver society will be advertising. Most of the industry will have to do an abrupt about-face. Yet no single firm need be hurt. The demand that advertising services be informative means only that advertisers will shift from sham to substance. Better than all others, advertisers are equipped to change tack when a new direction is called for.

Whenever an industry, or a business, does suffer there will be potential for individual suffering as well. Workers may have to be retrained or relocated. For many, adaptation will be difficult, but for most, it will not be necessary. A diverse economy will need diverse skills.

But aside from possible economic pains, the transition to a conserver society will not adversely affect individuals, with the rare exceptions of a tiny but growing minority that gags whenever it breathes fresh air.

Legislation passed under a conserver society will not foreclose future options; it will strive for diversity, give thought to a better balance, leave room for negotiations. Sun rights guaranteeing homeowners access to the sun will not mean the end of skyscrapers. Access to the sun can be negotiated by a developer on the same basis as any other property right. But it does give the homeowner the option not to sell. If he depends on the sun to heat his home, or to grow his plants, or to wake him up in the morning, it will be his right.

Individual rights can't help but be enhanced in a conserver society. As business diversifies, as it decentralizes, as it has fewer and fewer vested interests to protect, it will be able to exercise less political power. Other perspectives will carry a little more weight, the democratic process will run a little more democratically.

Setting up a conserver society in Canada will have its share of traumas, but that in itself is not seen by many to be the primary problem: the international ramifications are real. Setting up a conserver society in a non-conserving world, going it alone until the United States and others follow suit, will require a courage that can only come from conviction in the benefits of conserver policies and confidence in there being no other feasible course.

22   *Going It Alone*

NO MATTER HOW well a conserver society might work domestically, its test will come in fitting into a world framework. Politically, it must adjust to existing agreements: conserver policies must be seen to be fairminded and not designed to harm any particular country or philosophy.

Economically, a conserver society mustn't unfairly deny other countries our markets, or access to our resources. Nothing invites retaliation more surely than raising artificial trade barriers, either by slapping taxes on foreign goods entering the country or placing quotas on goods exported to us. Tariff and other trade barriers are discriminatory: they are designed to protect domestic industries by making foreign goods less competitive, or less accessible. They create a double standard: one for ourselves and one for our trading partners. It is the double standards that invariably lead to friction.

Almost every country in the world uses one form of trade barrier or another, and Canada is no exception. The international body that polices world trade has 850 examples of non-tariff barriers alone that countries believe to be unfair. But a conserver society would not need to depend on artificial trade barriers. Once true Canadian standards are set the trade barriers become natural ones, based on efficiency rather than expediency.

A pretty-looking product that is difficult to recycle could

have a remarkably high disposal tax added in to the initial purchase price; a product that costs little to buy but a lot to maintain won't look the bargain when its life-cycle costs are revealed.

Any company, any country would be free to compete for the Canadian market on an equal basis with Canadians, but only those meeting our particular needs would be successful. In areas where Canadian manufacturers are not involved, the foreign firms that best happen to meet our needs will prosper; in areas where Canadian manufacturers are producing for their home market, the firms that will meet our needs best will tend to be Canadian.

Many foreign-controlled firms will decide the Canadian market is worth producing for. They might be conserver-oriented themselves, or in need of diversification, or have developed too much good will here to merely pack up and leave. When these foreign-controlled companies compete on the same basis as Canadian-controlled firms, they will do as well as ours and prosper.

But they won't be prospering at the expense of our economy. Unlike typical branch-plant operators, in which innovations discovered in Canada are shipped to head office for development, the innovations of our conserver society will be particularly applicable to our needs. (An example might be Westinghouse. About 90% of its exports from Canada are already based on technologies researched and developed in Canada.) More of the fruits of Canadian research will stay on our soil to be developed here; our foreign investment will finally be providing us with long-term benefits from our benefactors.

While all these factors will be acting to progressively reduce our overall imports, our increasingly-efficient products will find increasing numbers of applications in other countries with similar needs to ours. The dismal record of our manufacturing industries will be righted, our huge balance-of-payments deficit in manufactured goods will start to decline and eventually become a surplus. The decline in employment we're experiencing in manufacturing—every month there are a staggering 10,000 fewer jobs than the month before—will reverse itself as manufacturing shakes off its historic weak-sister stereotype.

Partially offsetting the progressive increases in manufacturing exports will be progressive decreases in our exports of non-renewable resources—those increasingly scarce and precious commodities that can only be sold once. Oil exports have already been cut back and will soon, for all practical purposes, cease. Exports of natural gas are no longer being negotiated on traditional standards, but on a swap basis. Instead of price being the determining factor, what we give away today we expect to get back tomorrow.

If Canada wanted to act in a crude and uncompromising manner, it could afford to ban all exports of non-renewable raw resources until conditions are right. All the iron, all the copper, all the nickel, all the uranium, and all the other ores, concentrates, and scrap we ship out total about $3 billion per year, or a small fraction of the savings a conserver society would accumulate. But an abrupt arbitrary policy such as this would cause corporate and human suffering at home while creating chaos in those countries that depend on our resources for their own survival.

Canada, as a leading supplier of many resources and the fifth largest exporter of minerals and metals in the world, must ensure an orderly international transition. The total costs of some minerals—when social and environmental expenses are included—may jump dramatically in price. (The real rise in price will only be higher for our trading partners. Domestically, the price hike is really a different accounting system—instead of paying for social and environmental costs after the fact, as we have been, we'll be paying them at the time of purchase. But our exports didn't previously include all the costs. When they are included, they become new costs for importing countries.)

These rises must be phased in, both as a warning and buffer to others, and as an aid in our own transition. In practice, though, because other factors of production weigh far more heavily, higher prices for most minerals will not be difficult to absorb. Primary minerals equal only 3% of the cost inputs to new construction, 1.1% to household appliances, 0.3% to food and 0.9% to automobiles.

The country that will be most affected by Canada becoming

a conserver society is the United States. It accounts for about one third of our total energy and mineral exports, and fully half of our total non-fuel mineral exports. Indications are it will fare well. The United States is already showing an admirable ability to cut back on its own reliance on natural resources. Despite large increases in fuel prices since 1973 the United States' proportion of Gross National Product spent for all natural resources has been declining and is now only 6%.

A great bulk of Canada's exports has always been of the renewable variety. Our wood products, agriculture, livestock, even hydro-electricity, will continue to serve important global functions to the benefit of all. In the transition to a conserver society, to a conserving world that is totally regenerative, renewable resources will play an increasingly large role. Certain industries, such as pulp and paper, will have initial pollution-abatement hurdles to overcome, but these hurdles will have to be overcome world-wide, creating no major changes in international competitive positions. Rapidly accelerating renewable technologies will benefit those countries that first apply them— they will benefit the first conserver countries. Going it alone in a non-conserving world, far from presenting innumerable obstacles will offer only innumerable opportunities that will be easier to harvest in virgin territory than in areas that have been depleted.

Canada has tried many times in the past to become independent, to go it alone in the face of much foreign domination. Previous efforts have failed because they've been based on either short-sighted anti-Americanism, or futile dreams of buying back our country with no evident means of buying it, or outright plans of expropriating foreign concerns without regard for international ramifications.

A conserver society will assert itself, not by being anti-anyone but by being pro-Canadian; not by paying market prices to buy back foreign-controlled companies but by changing the market to encourage all companies in Canada to respond to Canadian needs; not by arbitrarily expropriating the efforts of others but by building our own nation through our own best efforts.

23 *The Freedoms of Conservation*

THERE IS GREAT refuge in numbers. Cars may kill 50,000 North Americans each year, we are told, but what about the millions of people who benefit from owning and enjoying their own vehicles? How relevant is it that 150,000 workers die each year from occupation-related diseases when the other 99.9% of the workforce prospers so profoundly? Why dwell on the 10% who are unemployed instead of emphasizing the 90% who are gainfully employed? These are merely the prices we pay for prosperity.

We have become used to thinking in terms of trade-offs. Do we penalize the power-boater, whose pollution kills the fish in a lake, or the fisherman, whose pleasure comes at the expense of the lover of big power boats? Do we opt to build more roads to reduce traffic congestion, when those roads will only encourage more people to drive, leading to more congestion; or do we expand public transit, which often leads to higher bus fares and encourages people to turn to the auto? Do we stop urban decay through funds raised by higher taxes, which will scare business investment away from the community and lead to more urban decay; or do we offer concessions to attract more business which will only speed urban decay and encourage people to move away from the city, which becomes bad for business?

These seeming contradictions have become inextricably part

of our system. At every turn we confront a paradox that para-
lyzes effective action, pitting one side against another, leaving
both sides losers in the long run. The confrontations are becoming increasingly common as our present system continues
to unfold to its logical conclusion, and we become trapped in
our own logic.

As with any paradox, the fault lies in the premise. Accept
that two plus two is five and mathematics could tell you 2,000
plus 2,000 is 5,000. Accept that all significant inventions have
been already made (as the British did a century ago) and the
patent office can be closed. Accept that progress has a price (as
we now do) and we find the final tally won't add up.

Progress that has a price isn't progress—the benefit to one
part of the system becomes the loss to another. Progress with a
price is just another trade-off, just another contradiction in
terms that clouds the conscience and allows the unconsciona-
ble.

Any politician could solve the problem of inflation if he
didn't have to concern himself with unemployment. Or the
problem of pollution if society didn't mind continuing to pick
up the tab for industry. Or the problem of energy supply if
lack of capital wasn't a factor. It takes no power of intellect, no
degree of courage, no strength of purpose to achieve "progress" in one area at the expense of another. This progress has
magically fostered widespread agreement in society that we are
prosperous, that every form of economic growth is good, that it
is a sign of success that we now consume twice as much energy
per person as we did in the sixties. Coupled with these statisti-
cal successes is widespread agreement that we are not twice as
happy as we were in the 1960s, that our society is far from
functioning as well as it should be, that our economy is somehow out of control. And we remain captives of the conclusion
that the way out is more of the way in.

Man has always dreamed of eliminating the drudgery in his
life. Machines were made to bear our burdens for us, systems
devised to carry away our sewage, entertainments devised to
stimulate our imaginations. We used capital and energy to
further our creative goals. We became so good at it that more

and more of our efforts became concentrated in furthering the use of capital and energy. And then somewhere along the way we forgot why we were furthering the use of capital and energy. We began using them to replace not only drudgery but creativity, to replace not only a source of unhappiness but a source of happiness. Our intellect turned on itself and capital now replaces thought.

The architect who once built homes to individual needs has been replaced by the developer who builds the same home for every individual's needs. It becomes overdesigned for some, underdesigned for others, inappropriate for almost all. The same design makes do for Windsor, which experiences disconcerting heat in summer, as it does for Whitehorse, which faces discouraging cold in winter, as it does for Halifax where the wind whistles through its walls.

Where we once matched resource use to available resources, such as in energy where 50 years ago different parts of our country ran on windmills, hydro-electricity, wood, coal, water-power—whatever was was locally available and appropriate—we are now trying to match one resource—electricity—to all available uses. Where we once placed value in using our resources well we now place value in not having to think about the use of what we have. The freedom to think has been replaced with the freedom not to think.

It will soon become clear that the freedom not to think is a luxury not worth relishing. We cannot long go on selling what we have so thoughtlessly. As spendthrifts we will have a short history.

Were all of Canada's resources to be inventoried, were the value of all of our arable land ($60 billion), forests ($30 billion), energy resources ($300 billion), mineral deposits ($80 billion), public utilities ($60 billion), schools, universities, hospitals and public buildings ($300 billion) to be tallied, were all of our factories, mines, and oil wells ($300 billion) added in, were the railroads, highways, docks, and airports ($60 billion) accounted for as well—were all of our resources prudently sold off and were every Canadian to retire on the income, we would have about $920 billion to divide among the 23 million population, or about $40,000 each. Invested in a secure spot, say in U.S. Savings Bonds, the income of every Canadian would amount to $300 per month—well below the poverty line, and hardly worth boasting about.

Canadians, it is clear, are not ready to retire as a nation. We need to work a while yet before we rest on our laurels, and if we intend to remain Canadians, we should do the work here.

Raw resources are often worth only 1% of their value before they've been processed into finished goods. In 1976, for example, 1.4 billion feet of timber was cut down in Canada for the pulp and paper industry. As standing timber it was worth $70 million, but after men and machines felled it, delimbed it and cut it to length it was worth $700 million, or ten times as much. When the pulpwood was converted to newsprint and wood pulp the value climbed to $7 billion, or 100 times as much.

Do this with the equivalent of all of our raw resources and the $40,000 asset of each Canadian becomes $4 million, the $300 per month income becomes $30,000 per month. Do this with the equivalent of one tenth or even one twentieth of our income and our wealth more than doubles, giving us the highest per capita income in the world, well ahead of the Danes. (Their average annual wage is $16,000 compared to our present $10,000)

But wealth without health, without pleasant surroundings, without security, without the leisure time to enjoy it, without a sense of purpose, without a moral society, without clean air and fresh water and a liveable environment, would be a hollow achievement. The modern Midas would not think it worth the price—he would recognize it as nothing more than another trade-off.

A conserver society would say "no more false trade-offs." No longer would we be told to choose between jobs and the environment—we can have both—or between quality and quantity—we can have both. No longer will it be a choice between them and us—there's enough for all if we release ourselves from the chains of our outdated policies, if we rationalize our short-term interests with our long-term goals, if we adopt the simple principles that we pay our own way, that we be responsible for our actions, that we think in terms of conserving. Conservation can help free us from the dilemma of where to allocate our scarce capital, open our options to free us from the possibility that if one thing goes wrong, everything goes wrong.

The dangers of an economy based entirely on nuclear energy, for example, go far beyond the very real threat of sabotage or nuclear proliferation. Going nuclear means we are tied to one form of energy for the future rather than a dozen—it means we have no flexibility should something go wrong. Going nuclear means it becomes the single biggest industry, equal in size to all the other industries combined. It means that if we lose just one industry we've lost half our entire industrial sector.

As with nuclear there are dangers with any centralized system. Weighing the risks and benefits will be what a conserver society will do best—it will base our growth, our life, our security on what we have, not what we might have. It will create an environment where information and efficiencies are paramount, where innovation can express itself, where alternatives are ever present, where we don't lock ourselves hopelessly into a single course, where we can be self-reliant and self-sustaining.

Aside from a brief period in human history, we have been conserver-oriented. The morality that accompanied this philosophy—a philosophy glorified by "waste not want not," "a stitch in time saves nine," "don't put all your eggs in one basket," "God helps those who help themselves," and countless others—expressed conserver themes.

The change from a conserver to our present consumer ethic did not come about because man became suddenly wasteful, suddenly unable to value his role in society. It occurred because the rules of the game appeared to change. When supplies are limitless there is no reason to conserve them. It would not occur to us to limit our oxygen intake, for example, because there is more than enough oxygen in air, and it is able to renew itself with sufficient efficiency for us to breathe at whatever rate we choose.

When energy, and many other resources, appeared as unlimited as oxygen, when it appeared there were no costs attached to their use, the reason to conserve evaporated. Now knowing these appearances were deceiving, the conserver ethic will reassert itself. We will go back to the original ground rules—the basic rules of survival—with a clearer purpose and understanding of the challenges ahead.

About Pollution Probe

Pollution Probe Foundation, one of Canada's leading environmental groups, has been at the forefront of many of this nation's central issues for over a decade. The establishment of air and water quality standards, the fights against DDT and phosphates, and the creation of initiatives in solar energy are all battles Probe has fought in and helped to win.

But the struggle against pollution and for sound energy policies has barely begun, and although fighting each cause issue by issue gets results, the overall progress is not easy to perceive when new problems are created faster than old ones are solved. The aim of Pollution Probe is to set up a framework in which new problems won't continually crop up because we will have set our house in order, and found that things can be done properly the first time.

Pollution Probe and Energy Probe, both projects of the Pollution Probe Foundation, could not exist without the support of those concerned about the directions in which this country is heading. The support of people like you has been crucial for the work we have done in the past, and is essential for the work we intend to do in the future.

Pollution Probe is a registered charitable foundation whose policies are set independently of any other institution. For more information write to:

Pollution Probe Foundation
University of Toronto
Toronto, Ontario
M5S 1A1

Sources, Notes, and Further Reading

1

Much of the information in this chapter comes from two excellent background studies prepared for this book by Professor Robert Tostevin of York University. These studies are available at the Pollution Probe Library. Further readings that might be fruitful include "The Recycler in America," published by the National Association of Recycling Industries, and Stuart Chase's *The Tragedy of Waste* (Macmillan, 1927).

3

Ironically, this chapter is guilty of perpetuating a myth of its own: Christopher Columbus, alas, was not entirely the hero history has made out. Scholars of his day were well aware that the earth was round, but unlike Columbus, they knew how far around it was. Columbus, looking at earlier, outdated charts thought circumnavigating the globe to be a brisker business than it was.

4

Updated reserve estimates can be found in the *Canadian Minerals Yearbook* and the *Canadian Mining Journal* (this chapter contains 1977 estimates). For more on the vulnerability of America's mineral supplies, see Mighdoll and Weisse, "We Need a National Minerals Policy" (*Harvard Business Review*, Sept./Oct., 1976). And for science fiction fans looking for the not-so-far future, "Mining Outer Space" and "An Electromagnetic 'Slingshot' for Space Propulsion" in *Technology Review* (June, 1977) contain more details on tapping the universe.

5

The February, 1977, issue of *Technology Review* was heavily relied upon for this chapter, particularly "Recycling in the Materials System" by Michael Bever, "Recycling the Junk Car" by Julius Harwood, and "The Indispensable (Sometimes Intractable) Landfill" by Stephen James.

6

The Florida fluorosis case is well documented and appears in many publications. I first came across it in the Spring, 1977, issue of *California Management Review*. The figures for the annual damage caused by air pollution were derived from the Environmental Protection Agency in the United States, and based on American data. They have been extrapolated to put them into a North American context. For a lively discussion of damage caused by cancer and the feasibility of improving testing procedures see *The American Economic Review* (Feb., 1977), particularly Kneese-Schulze ("Environment, Health and Economy—The Case of Cancer") and Dorfman ("Incidence of the Benefits and Costs of Environmental Programs").

7

The estimate of the additional tax that would be required on gasoline to equal society's subsidy to the automobile appears in the February, 1977, issue of *Technology Review*. It has been adjusted for inflation and, of course, because the Canadian gallon is larger than the American gallon. The $2,000 expense that the user of an electric space heater can force on society is conservative: according to the Science Council of Canada Report No. 27, the figure is actually closer to $3,000. And for more on the mining ability of plants, see *Scientific American*, May, 1973 for the Emanuel Epstein article, "Roots."

8

The Gyftopoulos and Widmer study referred to in this chapter, and a study by Ross and Williams were indispensable. Both can be found in issues of *Technology Review* (the latter, Feb., 1977, the former June, 1977). For a chattier version of these concepts, see the May, 1977, issue of *Fortune* magazine.

9

The Organization for Economic Co-operation and Development, the Science Council of Canada, and the Senate Special Committee on Science Policy have all produced reams of fascinating reports (most of them only mildly contradictory) on Canadian Science policy. Among my favourites were the OECD's "Reviews of National Science Policy —Canada," the Science Council's "Earth Sciences Serving the Nation," and "Innovation and the Structure of Canadian Industry," by Pierre L. Bourgault.

10

For another discussion of many of the research ideas expressed here, several of the Science Council of Canada's Reports (in particular No. 23 and No. 27) are excellent. For objective information about the Canadian nuclear industry try to avoid relying entirely on government and industry sources: The Canadian Coalition for Nuclear Responsibility (2010 Mackay St., Montreal) and Energy Probe offer wise and authoritative alternate views.

11

Many of the quotes from old business and trade publications also appear in Vance Packard's *The Wastemakers*, a book that is as remarkably relevant today as it was two decades ago. Planned Obsolescence was also of interest to the *Harvard Business Review* in the 1950s. "Opportunity for Persuasion" (September, 1958) is but one of many worthwhile articles.

12

For more on the efficiencies of products see *Technology Review*, (January, 1977). The product-life-cycle concept is nicely debunked in the January-February, 1976, *Harvard Business Review* article by Dhalla and Yuspeh and dozens of articles in *Quality Progress* list innumerable examples of life-cycle costing and the many benefits of quality goods and services.

13

For a far fuller view of the effects of advertising on production see John Kenneth Galbraith, particularly *The Affluent Society* and *The New Industrial State*. An expanded list of the monopolistic control four or fewer Canadian companies have in various industries can be culled from the Statistics Canada publication "Industrial Organization and Concentration in the Manufacturing, Mining, and Logging Industries."

14

Pollution Probe published an excellent study, "Packaging and the Environment" by John David Wood, on the weightiest (in pounds) form of unnecessary advertising: overpackaging.

15

A different treatment of Canada's capital concerns can be found in the comments of Ralph Sultan of the Royal Bank of Canada to the

National Research Council (May 3, 1978). Mason Gaffney's contribution to *Environmental Management* (Cambridge and Ballinger Press, 1976) might also be found intriguing.

16
Statistics Canada has a wealth of information on Canada's debts, interest payments, balance of trade deficits, current account deficits, and other tantalizing subjects related to our public debts. Enjoy yourself.

17
Money, by John Kenneth Galbraith, was the source for the historical information provided on inflation. The conventional causes of inflation are also discussed in Galbraith's *The Affluent Society* and *The New Industrial State*.

18
The $1 million investment required per job in our resource industries is often conservative, as noted in Science Council Report No. 26. More information on government confusion in education and employment policies is ably noted in the Lamontagne Report: "A Science Policy for Canada."

19
Though a half-century old, Bertrand Russel's *In Praise of Idleness* still has much to offer on the work ethic. In a Canadian context, much can be extracted from the Schneider-Solomon study, *A Practical Guide to Unemployment Insurance*.

20
Other implementation ideas can be found in the Science Council of Canada's Report No. 27, and in "Agenda for Action," published by a group of concerned citizens and available from the Science Council.

22
Specific questions on trade and tariff barriers can be directed to GATT (General Agreement on Tariff and Trade), 154 rue de Lausanne, 1211 Geneva 21, Switzerland. The percentages of cost inputs in production come from "The State of Our Mineral Position: A Provocation," by William Vogely (*Technology Review*, Oct./Nov. 1977).

23
Compiling an inventory of all our resources to determine the wealth of Canadians was the imaginative idea of Maurice Wayman in *Wealth and Welfare*. My imaginative idea was to steal it.

Index

CS

E S

SEQUENCES AND HYMNS

SEQUENCES AND HYMNS

CHIEFLY MEDIEVAL

BY

HENRY WILLIAMS MOZLEY

LONGMANS, GREEN, AND CO.

39 PATERNOSTER ROW, LONDON

NEW YORK, BOMBAY, AND CALCUTTA

1914

TABLE OF CONTENTS

[1] C. Coffin.   [2] Notker of St. Gall.   [3] J. B. de Santeuil.

[1] P. Abelard.   [2] Konrad of Gaming.

NOTE.—Of the Sequences here given, those that come from rhymed originals have been translated exactly or as nearly as may be in the metres of the Latin—as also the Hymns. The unrhymed or Notkerian Sequences (Nos. 3, 7, 8, 10, 23, 24, 27, 29), which have very much the same amount of rhythm as a Hebrew psalm or a Greek chorus, leave to a translator the responsibility of choosing the poetical form in which their English version should be presented.

The Sequences have mostly been taken from Dr. J. M. Neale's *Sequentiae ex Missalibus;* but some few will be found in Cardinal Newman's *Hymni Ecclesiae* or in Mone's *Lateinische Hymnen des Mittelalters.*

---

[1] Notker of St. Gall.

SEQUENCES AND HYMNS

1. SEQUENCE OF THE LIFE OF CHRIST

Quando noctis medium

HEN thro' the middle gloom
    The night in silence moved,
  Into the Virgin's womb
    God sent his Son beloved
To save us from our doom.

Wisd. xviii. 14.

Let every mouth praise God,
  For given is our new dower;
In fragrance Jesse's rod
  Hath borne its healing flower,
And heaven bedews the sod.

Here nature is beguiled,
  Her laws reversed are;
A Virgin undefiled
  Doth yet conceive and bear
A Son, the heavenly Child.

Is. vii. 14.

B

Behold God's human birth;
   In flesh the Light is veil'd,
Yet heaven resounds with mirth
   Salvation hath not fail'd
And peace returns to earth.

The Fruit succeeds the leaf,
   The star sends light divine,
From Egypt comes our Chief
   The Cross his royal sign;
The foe's fierce hour is brief.

In Bethlehem is found
   Our David, Salem's King;
Earth's kingdoms quake around
   When He whose praise we sing
On Gihon's throne is crowned.

1 Kings i. 45.

Death's cause there perisheth
   Where God hangs on the Wood;
Victor He yields his breath,
   For since the Cross hath stood
Death is destroyed by death.

The Sun in gloom that set
   Hath risen from the abyss;
In heaven He liveth yet,
   His work accomplish'd is
And cancelled our grave debt.

Beyond all skies He pleads
  The wounds of his great love,
His ever glorious deeds;
  And with the Church above
For us He intercedes.

Grant us Salvation's boon
  O Father ever blest,
Thro' all the merits won
  By Him Thou lovest best
Thy sole-begotten Son.   AMEN.

2. AN EVENING HYMN IN ADVENT

Statuta decreto Dei

T length the time by God's command
Appointed draweth nigh at hand:
Bought by so many years' delay
Shines forth from heaven the expected
day.

By Adam's deadly sin his race
Lies prostrate and bereft of grace,
And thro' long ages languisheth
In darkness and the shade of death.

The second death its victim claims
In wrath and everlasting flames;
That fearful looking for of doom
When the all-righteous Judge shall come.

O who the blessings can recall
Lost in such overwhelming fall?
What hand sufficient remedy
For wounds so grievous e'er supply?

Thou Christ the Word of God alone
Descending from thy heavenly throne,
To thine own image canst restore
The strength and grace it had before.

Rain down ye heavens from above,   Is. xlv. 8.
And let the earth in fruitful love
Bud forth the Righteous One, and shew
Salvation to a world of woe.

O Word of God made Flesh, to Thee
Eternal laud and honour be,
Whom with the Father we adore
And Holy Ghost for evermore.   Amen.

3. FOR CHRISTMAS DAY

Ecce jam votiva

BEHOLD the waning year hath brought
 The birthday of our Lord and King;
Now let our voice again be taught
 The strains which hosts angelic sing.

Forth from his chamber Christ at length
 The expected Bridegroom comes to-day,
Rejoicing with a giant's strength
 To run his life's appointed way.

All glory be to God on high
 Sing forth the heavenly armies still;
Peace upon earth, let us reply,
 Peace upon earth, to men goodwill.

For lo, the centuries of time
 Are borne in mighty course along
And usher in the years sublime
 Predicted in the sibyl's song.

FOR CHRISTMAS DAY

The Virgin leads the age of gold, Virg. Pollio.
  The iron race is on the wane;
The world renews its youth; behold,
  The golden years return again.

The sun hereafter sheds its light
  And warmth from day to day increased;
The star of Balaam crowns the night
  And calls the children of the East.

Fulfilled is all that either race
  Spake of the Christ that was to be,
The Hebrew prophets, first in place,
  The Gentiles' feebler augury.

For now the ancient stains of sin
  Are purged from the sons of earth;
A living stock is grafted in
  By this most new and wondrous Birth.

Obedient to the Archangel's word
  The Virgin beareth sinlessly;
The closed portal is unbarr'd Ezek. xliv. 2.
  That Israel's God may pass thereby.

O Christ who clothedst for our sake
  Godhead in mortal nature thus,
Grant that we may in Thee partake
  The gifts which Thou has won for us.

4. SEQUENCE FOR THE CIRCUM-
CISION OF CHRIST

In sapientia disponens omnia eterna Deitas

IN his wisdom ordering all things well
the Eternal Deity
Saw and pitied us long bound in chains
of dire adversity.

Then from highest heaven the Angel on his secret
errand sped

Bearing earthward that the Father of his Son had
promised.

He the Virgin greeteth, saying, Thou shalt God
and Man conceive,

Primal cause of things created, born the nations
to relieve.

Nor delayed she long, but answered, Be it so, and
full of grace

Bore the Light the Church to lighten, bore the
Sun of Righteousness.

Upon the Gentiles Light hath shined,
Not on the proud ones of mankind.

Within a manger He is found
Whom neither earth nor heaven can bound.

The star its brilliancy doth shed
For Jesse's rod hath blossomed.

The Royal sages from afar
Bring gold and frankincense and myrrh.

Circumcision suffered He
Who was born to set us free.

He the Jordan's flowing tide
To our cleansing sanctified.

Him the Virgin offereth
Sacrifice to save from death.

Simeon in his arms at length
Beareth Israel's Hope and Strength.

By the Saviour's power outpoured
   Wine from water first hath come;
Sight is to the blind restored,
   Feet to lame, and voice to dumb.

None other unto us is given
Than God the Son, the King of heaven.

So let the courts celestial sing
The praise of their exalted King.   Amen.

5. SEQUENCE FOR THE EPIPHANY OF OUR LORD

Ad Jesum accurrite

ASTEN ye to Jesu's feet,
Hearts subduing as is meet
To the nation's new-born King;

Lo the Star proclaims your Lord,
Inward faith in full accord
Greets the Saviour of mankind.

Hither bring your choicest gift,
All your heart to heaven uplift
Free affection's offering;

This the gift of highest cost,
This the Saviour pleaseth most,
Dedication of the mind.

Gold your charity divine,
Myrrh your stern self-discipline,
Frankincense your yearnings bring.

Gold the King acknowledgeth,
Myrrh the Man who saves by death,
  Frankincense Divinity.

Israel, be not envious
Of the nations saved from loss
  Through the unfolded mystery.

Where the Shepherds knelt around,
Eastern sages faithful found
  Win the object of their search.

Christ who calls the Jewish race
Gives the Gentiles too a place
  All within one hovel poor.

Bethlehem is to-day become
Origin and native home
  Of the Universal Church.

In men's hearts may Jesus reign,
Making all rebellion vain,
  Spreading life for evermore.

6. AN EVENING HYMN IN PASSIONTIDE

Amorem sensus erige

OUR hearts' affection to thy praise
    Giver of pardon, raise;
In mercy purging us within
    From every stain of sin.

Thou Saviour most compassionate
    Knowest man's fallen state;
How weak his earthly substance is,
    How great his miseries.

Our secret thoughts are all revealed,
    No mind from Thee concealed;
Dispel afar by thy bright beams
    The world's deluding dreams.

Rich, Thou didst lay thy wealth aside,
    For us wast crucified;
O let the Fountain opened thus
    New life impart to us.

As pilgrims upon earth we roam;
　　Thou art our port, our home;
We mourn in exile, guide our way
　　Back to the courts of day.

Thou art Life's River; Charity
　　And Truth thirst sore for Thee;
Thrice blest thy people, who always
　　Adoring on Thee gaze.

Great is thy Love's Memorial, great
　　In heaven thy glorious state;
Which without end they magnify
　　Who lift their hearts on high.

Lord in the virtue of thy Name
　　Grant us to win the same;
In whom alone our works take root
　　And bear us worthy fruit.

All praise to God the Father be,
　　Jesu all praise to Thee,
Whom with the Spirit we adore
　　Now and for evermore.　　AMEN.

7. SEQUENCE FOR EASTER DAY

Haec est sancta solemnitas solemnitatum

HAIL Festival of festivals most glorious
    Crown'd with the triumph of the
    Crucified,
    Who in the power of the Cross vic-
    torious
And by the Blood from out his pierced side
Breaks down the strong man's empire, and re-
    deems us
    As on this Easter morn, this Day of days;
Therefore O Christ our King it well beseems us
    To join with choirs angelic in thy praise.

With favour look on us who here proclaim Thee
    Victorious, since to save our fallen race
Thou didst put off that glory which became Thee
    And to a death of shame Thyself abase.
Now all is past; the chains of hell are riven,
    Thou reignest o'er the nations gloriously;
Therefore rejoice we ransom'd and forgiven
    In this thy Rising, Son of God most High.
                    AMEN.

8. SEQUENCE FOR SUNDAYS AFTER EASTER

Rex Deus, Dei Agne

GOD and King, true Lamb of God;
   To Thee the Lion of Juda's tribe
Who trod'st the Cross's bitter road,
    All power and might we now ascribe.

By thine own Death, a death to sin
   A life to righteousness bestow
That we the fruit of life may win
   And all thy glorious wisdom know.

For since thy Blood hath quenched the ban
   Of the cherubic fiery sword,
Thou openest Eden's gate to man,
   Source of all healing, gracious Lord.

Gen. iii. 24.

New light in heaven, new peace on earth,
   Dismay in hell's abysmal deep;
While the twofold baptismal birth
   Of Law and Gospel here we keep.

I Cor. x. 2.

1 Cor. v. 7.

This is our passover indeed;
    The new is come, the old hath fled;
Rejoice, from leaven unholy freed,
    Quickened with Truth's unleavened bread.

The foe are drowned beneath the sea,
    The saving blood our lintels bear,
The victim slain, one household, we
    With fire and bitter herbs prepare.

With girded loins, with shoes on feet,
    With staff in hand, we take our way;
The Paschal Sacrifice we eat
    In whom our night is turned to day.

Purge us ev'n now with hyssop; sanctify
Our bounden service; make it worthier Thee;
Dry up the sea before us, draw therefrom

Job xli. 1.

With thy strong hook Leviathan our foe.
Then with thy chalice soothe and cheer us, Lord;

Ps. cx. 7.

Raise us, O Thou who drankest by the way
The brook of our deep sins; Victim and Priest
The winepress treading, join us to Thyself.
O Flower most fragrant of the Virgin Rod
O Lamp bedewed with the sevenfold oil
Of heavenly grace; fairer than milk or wine,
White as the lily, ruddier than the rose;

Since Thou with counsel of such clemency
Did'st condescend to aid our petty world
And be to us Prince and Redeemer, born
Thyself all sinless, neath the yoke of sin;
Therefore O Lord our Brother, by thy word
To Abraham's seed, in promise of the first
And final Resurrection, strengthen us
Immortal King, revive us by thy Blood
Who lay in our first parent Adam dead;
Unite our feeble members to thine own
Of power triumphant; grant us in Thyself
Eternal pastures, Thou our Passover.   AMEN.

C

9. HYMN FOR THE OCTAVE OF THE ASCENSION

Felix dies mortalibus

 HAPPY day for mortal men
  When by his Blood for sinners given
Our God in manhood entered in
  Thro' the long closed gates of heaven.

Whither our Head and Guide hath gone
  His members we will follow there,
If we in heart with Him are one
  With us his glory He will share.

He went, yet leaves us not alone
  Still present He his Spirit gives
And intermingled with his own
  Thro' all his mystic Body lives.

But O, that day of gloom and fear
  That day of terrible distress,
When He descending shall appear
  The Avenger of unholiness.

Sinless by sinners sentenced
   He then the Judge's seat shall take
Before whose face, to judgment led
   Shall his unrighteous judges quake.

To save us from our meed of death
   Death of His own free will He sought
Then O what vengeance threateneth
   Those whom God's Death shall profit naught.

Let those o'erwhelmed in mortal sin
   Avert the anger of their Lord
And ere too late in tears begin
   To quench the flames of their reward.

Jesu, Thou future Judge of earth
   Father and Holy Ghost to Thee
Ascribe we glory, praise and worth
   Now and throughout eternity.   Amen.

10. SEQUENCE FOR WHITSUNTIDE

Amor Patris et Filii

LOVE of God from God proceeding
　The Brightness of true hope and trust,
　　The Comforter of all,
　Unfailing Light the faithful leading
Reward long wished for of the just,
　Raiser of them that fall.
O Author of all fortitude
O Fountain of all sanctity
Giver of all beatitude
Lover of all integrity;
Almighty, all encompassing,
All sinless, ever pitying,
Whose strength and purity and worth
Transcend the loftiest thoughts of earth.
Hail, holiest, most beloved, best
Illuminator of the breast,
The way to Father and to Son
Through Thee alone by man is won.
Spirit of might and love
In whom we live and move,

Of sweetest influences
Unknown to carnal senses,
The medicine of every sin
In whom all health and joy begin,
Spirit of counsel pure
Spirit of wisdom sure
   Truth loving ever,
Finger of Hand divine
Bond of the Eternal Trine
   Lord and Lifegiver;
Who with his virtue fills
When, where and how He wills
   By his good pleasure;
Informs with breath of life,
Strengthens to win the strife,
   Gives lasting treasure.
Sublime beyond all thought,
Bounteous when humbly sought,
   Kind to deliver,
Comes He to-day to greet
The Church with counsel sweet
   Comes without measure;
Through whom from God on high
Descendeth plenteously
   Wisdom's pure river.   ALLELUIA.

11. SEQUENCE OF THE HOLY TRINITY

Vox clarescat mens purgetur

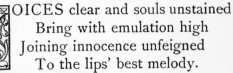OICES clear and souls unstained
  Bring with emulation high
 Joining innocence unfeigned
  To the lips' best melody.
Father Son and Spirit praise we
 With exultant hearts and minds,
To the Three one anthem raise we
 Whom one simple Essence binds.

God the Father self-existent,
 God the sole begotton Son,
Love of God in Them subsistent
 Are in very Nature One.
Three in Person unconfounded
 One in Godhead, One in Name,
One in Majesty unbounded
 In all attributes the same.

Each in his own function truly
 From the Two distinguished is;

But no human mind can duly
    Fathom such deep mysteries.
Father Son and Spirit ever
    Aid us in our ghostly strife
Us from Satan's bondage sever
    Bring us to eternal Life.   AMEN.

12. SEQUENCE OF THE HOLY EUCHARIST

O Panis dulcissime

COME Thou sweetest Bread of Heaven
To thy faithful people given
  As the soul's best nourishment;
Gentlest Lamb the world e'er saw
Paschal Victim of the law,
  Sacrifice from Heaven sent.

Undecaying, Flesh divine,
Who beneath the outward sign
  Veiled art celestially;
By the sevenfold sustenance
  Of thy Spirit's providence
  Satisfy us bounteously.

Eaten yet remaining whole
Thou the true receiver's soul
  Quick'nest everlastingly;
And the taint of sinful earth
By thy gift of wondrous worth
  Purifiest graciously.

Us to thine own Self unite,
Fortify us by thy might
   Worthily to taste of Thee;
So that by thine aid we may
Carnal longings chase away
   Dwelling with Thee holily.

So refreshed with heavenly Food
Drinking of that precious Blood
   Which Thou shed'st so lovingly;
Be we though among the least
Called to banquet at Thy Feast
Unto all eternity.   AMEN.

13. SEQUENCE FOR THE CON-VERSION OF SAINT PAUL

Tuba Domini Paule maxima

IGHTIEST Clarion thou of our Lord
Paul, on our foes let thy thunder be
pour'd
Gather the citizens, scatter the horde.

Thou of the Gentiles' Apostles the first,
Full of all wisdom divinely rehearsed,
Acts ix. 15. Vessel of grace to extinguish our thirst.

Gen. xlix. 27. At morn a Benjamin, ravenous of mood,
Thou did'st at even distribute the food
Wherewith the life of the world is renew'd.

Job xxxix. 10. Once the untameable unicorn thou
Whom the great Husbandman yoked to his plough
Breaking and harrowing earth's valleys now.

He the unjust steward well doth requite
Luke xvi. 8. Largely commending his anxious foresight,
Now become zeal for the children of light.

Laud to the Three everlastingly One,
Laud to the Captain of armies, the Son,
Laud to the Father and Spirit be done.

14. HYMN FOR THE CONVERSION OF
SAINT PAUL

LORD who fulfillest thus anew
  Thine own blest dying prayer,
That they who know not what they do
  May in thy ransom share;

When foes thy Church's power defy,
  Or slight thy sacred Word,
Or Thee, true God and Man, deny,
  Grant them conversion, Lord.

Grant that the light may round them shine,
  That, set from error free,
They in thy Word the Truth divine,
  Thee in thy Church may see.

That so when our brief time is done
  We may with them adore
The Father and coequal Son
  And Spirit evermore.   AMEN.

15. SEQUENCE FOR THE PRESENTA-
TION OF OUR LORD

Ave plena gratia

MARY hail to thee we sing
   Who within thine arms dost bring
      God, to God self-consecrate;
    Jesu, Love beyond compare,
Grant that I may meet Thee there
  Waiting at thy Temple gate.

Now thy house receives its Lord
Angel hosts around Him poured;
  Heaven hath nothing more divine;
God in human form arrayed
Dowers with grace the Mother Maid;
  O how rich his earthly shrine.

Lo the altar breathes delight,
Lo to-day the morning rite
  Is with joy accomplished.
But the evening sacrifice
From the Cross with woe shall rise
  And with wailing for the dead.

This our Offering is indeed,
Whose availing work we plead
   Reconciled to God on high;
Now no more astray are we,
Newly bound O Lord to Thee
   We in Thee both live and die.

Let thy servants now depart,
Let them see Thee as Thou art,
   Nothing here enslaves our eyes;
If Thou bid'st us stay below
Grant us with thy Child to grow,
   Grant in Him at last to rise. AMEN.

16. SEQUENCE FOR THE ANNUN-
CIATION OF OUR LADY

Salve salve sancta parens

HAIL, all hail, O sacred Mother
By the Archangel's word no other
Than the Word dost thou conceive:
Thou our nature's bounds forsaking
For thy Son God's Son art taking
Virgin Mother, second Eve.

As the dew on wool descendeth,
As the sun his ray extendeth
Through the glass, and works no ill;
So the Father's power all-holy
Shadows o'er that Mother lowly
Gloriously a Virgin still.

By the ever closed portal   Ezek. xliv. 2.
Enters He whom nature mortal
Cannot, dareth not oppose;
But adores Him wonder-laden,
Hears the name of Mother-Maiden,
Little yet its meaning knows.

Gabriel's Ave, mystic greeting,
Backward Eva's name repeating
  Turns her woe to joyfulness:
By whose word of restoration
Give we thee our salutation
  Hail thee Mother, full of grace.

17. HYMN FOR THE FEAST OF SAINT PETER

ILLAR of holy Church,
Chief of the Saints of God
Who upwards from his fall
The path of suffering trod;

Not once nor thrice alone
Did Peter mourn his sin,
Striving with tears the fruit
Of penitence to win.

Not once nor thrice alone
Wrought he with power for men,
In gold and silver poor,
Rich in the talents ten.

Not once nor thrice alone
Have we denied Thee, Lord;
O that with holy grief
Our tears like his were poured;

D

That strengthened in his faith
Through prayer and Eucharist
We too might live and work
And die in Thee, Lord Christ.

Yet grant, though far below
The Apostolic throne,
Some rest at thy dear Feet,
Some mansion with thine own.   AMEN.

18. SEQUENCE FOR THE TRANS-
FIGURATION

De parente summo natum

GOD the Word, from ages distant
   With the Father coexistent,
     Uncreate eternally;
   Such his honour and condition
By no favour or permission
   But his own essentially;

He, that Word, mankind befriending
Threatened sore by woe unending,
   Earth in servant's likeness trod;
And was made a creature newly
Human laws observing duly
   Yet remaining very God:

So of natures twain possessor
That the greater in the lesser
   Was without pollution clad;
Nor was lesser lost in greater;
Both the creature and Creator
   From their union honour had.

Of this wondrous Incarnation
  In the Lord's Transfiguration
  Proof we have invincible:
Wherein is to us revealed
That which was awhile concealed
  Neath the mortal Body's veil.

Doomed to death for our offences
That same Flesh its evidences
  Of a glorious power displays;
For his raiment's snowy whiteness
And the cloud's unearthly brightness
  Speak the Word's transcendent praise.

And the Voice its witness bearing
Faithfully from heaven declaring
  Him the well beloved Son,
Gives us testimony certain
That the Flesh was but the curtain
  Under which the Godhead shone.

In one Christ by faith supernal
We acknowledge God Eternal
  And the Virgin Mary's Son;
In one Person Him receiving,
Of two natures Him believing
  Joined in perfect union.

Lo the Stone which then rejected 1 Peter ii. 7.
By the Jews, but now elected
   Is become the corner's head;
Clothed with Light all light excelling
Fraught with Deity indwelling
   As the Apostles witnessed.

With Thee, Lord, in full fruition
Of thy Beatific Vision
   Grant us evermore to dwell;
To our heritage O lead us
Who thro' Jordan did'st precede us
   As did Joshua Israel.   AMEN.

19. SEQUENCE OF THE CROWN OF THORNS

Si vis vere gloriari

IF thou aright would'st glory
    If thou would'st win the prize
Bestowed by God Almighty
    On those who heavenward rise;
Learn thou his Crown to honour
    Learn in his steps to tread
Who faint and bleeding bore it
    On his most sacred Head.

The Monarch of creation
    This crown did condescend
To sanctify and wear it
    At his Life's bitter end.
In this his helmet fought He
    With this in battle stood
Against the ancient foeman
    Triumphant on the Rood.

This then the Warrior's helmet,
    The Victor's laurel this,

The Diadem Imperial,
  The Pontiff's mitre is;
Of thorns it first was platted
  To shame and pain untold;
But lo, that Head most holy
  Hath touched and made it gold.

The Virtue of Christ's Passion
  Hath mightily gone forth,
And shed on that rude circlet
  Its gifts of countless worth.
That Passion which enduring
  The hard and thorny wood
Those doomed to death eternal
  Hath satisfied with good.

Of evil it is platted
  To us who slight his Word;
The thorny points deep wound us
  Which wounded once our Lord.
But when our sins are purged
  And we in grace abide,
Behold, the crown is golden,
  The points are turned aside.

O kind, O righteous Jesu
  Grant to us all thy power

That we may be victorious
   In death's approaching hour.
So fashion Thou our conduct
   In this our mortal strife,
That we the crown may merit
   Of everlasting life.

20. SEQUENCE OF THE SAME

Florem spina coronavit

THE thorn hath crowned the Flower now
Hath crowned its own Creator's brow,
 The Flower of Mary born;
The Flower from whom the rugged wood
Alone receiveth all its good,
 The Flower without a thorn.

Though wounded by its cruel points
He the invading thorn anoints
 With oil of holiness;
The Tree of Life bears living boughs
Whence healing to the nations flows
 Under the sting's distress.

More rich than gold, more fair, more good,
This in the Lamb's lifegiving Blood
 Doth blossom as the rose;
A mighty helmet it is made
Whereby in man's estate arrayed
 Our God doth foil His foes.

Ex. xxv. 10.

More fragrant than the shittim wood
Of which was made the ark that stood
   In the most holy place;
Strive we Christ's Crown to honour so
That He may ours on us bestow
   After this day of grace. AMEN.

21. SEQUENCE FOR THE EXALTA-
TION OF THE CROSS

Ave Crucis dulce lignum

AIL wood of Cross most sweet
    Standard of triumph fair
    Who wast alone accounted meet
    Thy Lord and God to bear:
On thee uplifted Christ
Hath vanquish'd death, thereunto born,
  As Isaac sacrificed
  To save our race forlorn.

  Hail sinners' stair, whereby
  Our Saviour did ascend
That so to angel choirs on high
  Man too his way might wend.
  On thee was life restor'd
By the Life-giver, David's Son,
  And through our humbled Lord
  A world from ruin won.

  Hail sign of doctrine deep,
  Emblem of royal sway,

On thee the Shepherd of the sheep
   Purged all their sins away.
   He be our Shepherd good
Our Guide to realms of light on high
   Who willed with his own Blood
   The Cross to sanctify.   AMEN.

22. HYMN TO THE GUARDIAN ANGEL

Salve mi Angelice

AIL my guardian Angel, hail
  Spirit ever blessed,
Who of light within the veil
  Fully art possessed:
Thou of God Almighty hast
  Beatific vision,
Sweet for ever to the taste
  Unalloyed fruition.

When the rebels proud were cast
  Into death undying,
Thee did God establish fast
  Heavenly grace supplying;
In thy ways preserved thee
  Angel true and tender,
And appointed thee to be
  My weak soul's defender.

Therefore I on bended knee
  Bow myself before thee,
And upraising suppliantly
  Heart and hands implore thee

That with ever watchful art
   Thou to-day would'st aid me,
Lest the adversary's dart
   Subtly should invade me.

May my body from distress
   Be by thee protected,
Be all stain of wickedness
   From my mind rejected;
Everywhere and always speed
   From the foe to hide me
And in thought and word and deed
   Be at hand to guide me.

Cleanse all past and present faults
   From my heart's intention,
And when evil next assaults
   Grant thy intervention
O befriend and care for me
   Comfort me in trouble,
Purge, enlighten perfectly,
   Bid my zeal redouble.

Pray that I remission find
   Of the Judge's sentence,
So to share my joy of mind
   On my true repentance.

Living as shall please Him best
   Unto my life's closing,
All my longings now at rest
   All on Him reposing.

In the hour of death bestow
   Thy true consolation,
Guard me from the watchful foe,
   Bid me take my station
Where the blissful choirs among
   In God's courts attending
I may join the praises sung
   To His Name unending.

23. SEQUENCE FOR THE FEAST OF ALL SAINTS

Resultet tellus et alta coelorum machina

ET Heaven's exalted sphere
    And earth re-echo clear
      The Eternal Father's praise who rules
        the sky;
  To whom the angelic throng
  Raise their harmonious song
In the celestial palaces on high:
  So also let us here to-day
With tuneful voice before Him our thanksgivings
    lay.

  The choir of all the Blest
  In Paradisal rest
To Him full tribute of devotion yields
  There the new song they raise
  In Christ their Captain's praise
Treading the pure flowers in the dewy fields;
  And clad in white, with laurel crown'd
Follow the Lamb their Guide where'er his steps
    are found.

For they the alluring gleams
  Of this world's short-lived dreams
Despising, yearn'd for joys of highest heaven;
  Through the blest Spirit's power
  Who his bright gifts doth shower
Whereby to us immortal life is given;
  For He doth search our inmost part,
And from all taint of sin doth purify the heart.

He Consubstantial, One
  With Father and with Son,
For ever reigns in his high citadel;
  Where glowing with the sight
  Of that eternal Light
The companies of Saints in rapture dwell;
  The Majesty Supreme they view
Throned each in rank and order of precedence due.

The essential Unity
  And sacred Trinity
In glory everlasting they adore;
  Whereto when death is past
  God bring our souls at last
To worship Him with Angels evermore;
  For in Him all his Saints rejoice
And we with all redeemed raise our triumphant
        voice. ALLELUIA. AMEN.

E

24. SEQUENCE FOR ALL SOULS' DAY

De profundis exclamantes

UT of the deep, O Christ, we cry
   Thee,
   Lord hear our voice in heaven thy dwel
   ing place;
For those departed in thy faith and fear
Thy suppliant Church intreats; do Thou give ea
Incline to them the brightness of thy Face
And grant them rest. All sinners though we be
And may not stand if Thou should'st be extrem
To notice aught amiss, yet let to-day
The salutary Sacrifice avail
For those whom Thou did'st by thy Blood redeer

That which Thou offered'st to the Father, may
We offer it, for them effectual
That Thou may'st in thy pity set them free.
For by the law of their condition, they
Now can abide before Thee; therefore turn
O Lord, their bondage—Now they hope in The
Then draw them forth up to thy palace gate.

In Thee they hope and trust, for Thee they yearn,
Morning and evening yearn they, day and night,
And in the deep thy saving health await.
Then let them Lord thy bounteous pity learn:
Be Thou to them full confidence and might
And purge them as we pray from every stain.
Lo now thy Mother lo thy Saints intreat;
Let not their fervent prayers be spent in vain
But hear their intercessions, as is meet.
Kind Jesu, glorious King, who on the Cross
Once lifted shew'dst for sinners such great love,
Hear now our congregation's earnest prayers
Of thy compassion. Save them from all loss,
Break through the gates of death, foil Satan's
        snares,
And let the souls attain eternal joys above.

25. HYMN FOR THE OCTAVE OF ALL SAINTS

Adesto summa suavitas

COME sweetness Thou without alloy
    The Son's and Father's Love,
That by thy comfort perfect joy
    May fill us from above.

'Twas Thou did'st overshadow her
    Who the new Adam bore,
By whom from bonds of death we were
    Released evermore.

Thou mad'st the Apostles' heart to burn
    With gift of lore unpriced,
That in the scriptures they might learn
    The mystic wealth of Christ.

And by thy counsel it was shewn
    That Gentiles led by faith
Should Him acknowledge whom his own
    Had scorn'd and put to death.

Thou gav'st the Martyrs strength to mock
   At every menace hurl'd
By persecutors of the flock
   The princes of the world.

Thou gav'st the Doctors of the Church
   Wisdom's celestial ray
To chase in their enlightened search
   Error's foul mists away.

That gift of thine we need to use
   The oil of piety
We pray Thee thro' our hearts diffuse
   O Lord abundantly.

Lest in the Judgment Day we fall
   With those Thou wilt reject
Let godly fear ensure our call
   To join the souls elect.

From every mouth thy praise be heard
   Sole source of grace and meed,
Who from the Father and the Word
   Dost evermore proceed.   AMEN.

26. SEQUENCE FOR FEASTS
OF APOSTLES

Cujus laus secundum nomen

OD the Lord whose praise and glory
    Is according to his Name,
Who his ever righteous judgments
    Doth thro' all the world proclaim;

Him the wicked conscience-stricken
    As his Judge with fear doth own;
Him the righteous loves adoring
    Ransomed by his grace alone.

These of old were counsels hidden
    In the depths beyond our sight;
But the Wisdom of the Father,
    God of God and Light of Light,

Now hath visited his people
    Now hath come amongst his own
And the secrets of the Godhead
    Hath to men as Man made known.

He the mysteries, aforetime
 Under figures dim conceal'd,
To the lowly and the foolish
 Of the world hath now reveal'd;

Whom He hath exalted highly,
 Clothed with power and dignity,
That to every land and nation
 They his witnesses might be.

They are firmaments containing
 Mysteries celestial,
They the clouds abounding ever
 Whence the rains of doctrine fall.

They the Church's deep foundations,
 They her gates and corridors,
They the pedestals and pillars
 Reared on which she upward soars;

Lanterns of the Word, diffusing
 All around their brilliance;
Salt of earth, the earth preserving
 By their acts of continence.

They the shepherds of the sheep-folds
 Keeping well their flocks from blame,
They the teachers, guiding rightly
 Their disciples' hearts and aim.

Therefore by their intercession
  Grant that we at thy right hand
May with them receive our portion
  In the heavenly Fatherland. AMEN.

27. SEQUENCE FOR FEASTS OF EVANGELISTS

Regnum tuum regnum omnium seculorum

LORD thy power is everlasting
Thy dominion knows no bound;
This the living creatures herald
Full of eyes within, around;
Man and lion, calf and eagle,
Scanning mysteries profound.

Mark and Luke and John and Matthew
Preach the Word in tones allied;
By whose form and in whose language
Thou O Christ art signified;
Thou in thy most gracious Manhood
And the Church thy royal Bride.

Thou art Man, the Son of Mary;
Thou wert slain on Calvary,
Lion in thy Resurrection,
Eagle soaring to the sky:
And the Church's children also
Are exemplified thereby.

They are men, thy members; daily
  Crucify the flesh with Thee;
They endued with lion's courage
  Make the ghostly tempter flee;
On the very Sun as eagles
  Fix their gaze adoringly.

Hab. iii. 8.

In thy chariot of salvation
  Thine Evangelists have place;
They the wheels, fourfold the timbers
  Fashioned of the Cross of Grace;
Thou O Lord Thyself art Rider,
  Urge thy horses in the race.

Is. lvx. 20.

From the mire of our transgressions
  From the troubled sea of sin
Raise us by thy power Almighty,
  Stay thy chariot, take us in;
Till the goal of peace eternal
  Till the heavenly Land we win.

Where with all thy faithful people
  Praise we Thee with one accord,
Singing with those living creatures
  Holy, Holy, Holy, Lord;
May their eyes unresting teach us
  Watchful care for such reward. AMEN.

28. SEQUENCE FOR SAINTS' DAYS

Supernae Matris gaudia

ET forth O Church exultingly
The joys of Salem throned on high;
And keeping yearly holiday
Long for the feast that lasts for aye.

O let the mother aid her child   Gal. iv. 26.
Beleaguer'd in this desert wild;
And guards celestial here below
Join ranks with ours against the foe.

The world, the flesh, and Satan wage
Their warfare with incessant rage,
And by their ghostly onsets wrest
Away the Sabbath of the breast.

This triple league with hatred sore
Our holy festivals abhor,
And joined in kindred union strive
The peace of God from earth to drive.

All here is with confused noise
All hopes and griefs, all fears and joys:
Rev. viii. 1.
Not one half hour to us is given
To taste the eternal calm of heaven.

How blest that city throned above
In feast day of perpetual love;
How sweet those courts celestial are
Untouched by mortal toil and care.

No languor, no old age they know
No fraud, no terror of the foe,
But one the voice of them that sing
One glow all hearts illumining.

The citizens angelical
In threefold hierarchy all
Do homage with devotion high
To the One Trinal Sovereignty.

Unfaltering they fix their glance
On his unveiled countenance,
And Him insatiate adore,
Whom to enjoy they thirst the more.

The Fathers ranged on either hand
According to their honour stand;
The mists of earth away are roll'd,
And in his light they light behold.

The Saints of God whose high estate
We here to-day commemorate
Now face to face eternally
Their King in all his beauty see.

May we to their high glory rise
Out of these present miseries,
Helped by their prayer to their reward,
Saved by the grace of Christ our Lord.

AMEN.

29. SEQUENCE FOR FEAST OF DEDI-CATION OF A CHURCH

Psallat tuae gloriae ecclesia Mater illibata

NOW let the Church our Mother being
free
From any spot or wrinkle, sing
Lord, to thy glory; offering
Due thanks for this thy earthly house, by Thee
Approved an offshoot of the heavenly courts
For praise of heaven's great King, whereto resort
The Christian company; by sacred rite
And by perpetual light
Emulous of her, the City wherein lies
No shadow; in its bosom cherishing
Bodies of Saints who live in Paradise.
Such house may God in mercy long protect.
Here grace brings forth new offspring of the elect
Begotten by the Spirit; angels tend
Their fellow citizens; Christ's Body here
Is duly given. All ailments here have end;
Vanish transgressions of the penitent soul;
Ring songs of joy and peace, for heaven is near;
Voices of praise the Eternal Trinity extol.

30. BEFORE LAYING ON OF HANDS IN CONFIRMATION

Prayer for the Candidates

LORD who while yet a boy wast found
　　Within thy Father's house of prayer,
While listening sages all around
　　Wondered what child of God were
　　　　there;

Then wentest forth, and yet again
　　Wast subject unto earthly rule,
Learning thro' years of toil and pain
　　Thy guileless mind and heart to school;

Lo here thy children at thy shrine
　　Await in faith and hope and love
The Finger of the Hand divine
　　Thine own anointing from above.

As they to Thee their souls uplift
　　Obedient to thy dread commands,
So seal them with Thy Spirit's gift
　　Through touch of Apostolic hands.

Then send them forth to do thy will,
  With single-hearted trust in Thee,
Thee their sure Guide thro' good and ill,
  Their joy to all eternity.   AMEN.

31. AFTER LAYING ON OF HANDS IN CONFIRMATION

Response of the Confirmed

O do his blessed will
    Confirmed with his full strength,
To follow Him thro' good and ill
    And win his joy at length;

Can nobler task than this
    To human powers be given?
Why stay for dreams of earth? why miss
    The imperious call from Heaven?

Soldiers of Christ, we own
    In Him our Lord and Chief;
His word our law, his smile alone
    Our stay in joy and grief;

His Cross our beacon set
    To point the road He trod,
Who paid for us the eternal debt
    And ransomed us to God.

F

And may that Spirit blest
Who poureth from on high
On those that gird them for the quest
His sevenfold sanctity;

May He in power and love
Go with us day by day;
Till to thy Father's house above
Thou call us Lord away.   AMEN.

32. FOR SCHOOLS: HYMN FOR THE BEGINNING OF THE SCHOOLTIME

GAIN to thy dear Name
 O Saviour Christ, we raise
 Even as before, though not the same
  Our fervent hymn of praise.

Fresh from the joy of home,
 Fresh from the converse sweet
Of loving hearts, again we come
 Our comrades here to greet;

And with them, Lord, to pay
 Due homage unto Thee
Who hast preserved us day by day
 From toil and trouble free.

As flows our river on,
 New waters but one river,
So we succeed to others gone
 Thine heritage for ever

Who now at duty's call
Resume our bidden task,
Trusting that Thou wilt give us all
The help we need to ask:

For growth of earthly lore,
For grace of industry,
And as Thou willest, more and more
Knowledge of self and Thee.

These mercies ask we, Lord,
Father and Blessed Son,
Who with the Spirit art adored
While endless ages run.   AMEN.

33. AT SCHOOLS: FOR THE LAST DAY OF THE SCHOOLTIME

THOU who know'st not time nor place
    nor change
Thou sole unchangeable, yet dost ordain
    To us thy creatures each his different
range,
His cup of weal and woe, his loss and gain;

Behold us here assembled in thy sight
Who ne'er can hope again with one accord,
None absent, all thy goodness to requite
With thanks and praise from eager hearts out-
    pour'd.

Anew for some will dawn their schoolboy days,
The various round of work and play; for some
The altered scene, the parting of the ways,
The fuller life of toil and hope is come.

Yet all are knit in love, or far or near,
To Thee and to each other; hence shall rise
From many tongues one voice of praise and prayer
On sea, on shore, in earth, in Paradise.

Only do Thou uphold us as we go
Or while we stay, where'er our lot be cast;
That they who now are parted here below
May meet, dear Lord, before thy throne at last.

34. HYMN OF NATIONAL THANKS-GIVING AFTER WAR

NOT unto us, O Lord,
   Not unto us be given
The praise that comes by man's award
   To those who well have striven.

Thine be the praise alone
   For all things come of Thee;
We do but reap where Thou hast sown
   Fulfilling thy decree.

1 Chron.
xxix. 14.

'Tis thine the arm to nerve;
   'Tis thine the heart to fire;
'Tis thine whate'er occasion serve
   Right judgment to inspire.

Thine are the issues, far
   Beyond all earthly skill;
The turns of chance, that make or mar
   According to thy will.

1 Kings xxii.
34.

Yet count it not for blame,
Deem not our boasting naught,
That we to our dear Mother's name
One honour more have brought:

That we rejoice to-day
In not unworthy pride,
And hope through Thee to strive alway
Our best, whate'er betide.

Lord of the hosts of heaven,
Lord of the wars of earth,
To Thee from our glad hearts be given
All honour praise and worth.

Ex. xv. 2;
Ps. xlvi. 9.

35. SEQUENCE FOR FOUNDER'S DAY AT ETON COLLEGE

YOUNG and old, lift up your voices,
　　To your Lord meet tribute bring,
Him in whom his Church rejoices
　　Ever lowly worshipping;
Christ your Master, Christ your Pastor
　　Christ of earth and heaven the King.

Praise him too, whose princely spirit
　　Christ in wisdom so refrain'd
That he gave us to inherit
　　'Neath the Palace where he reign'd
Royal treasure passing measure,
　　Knowledge high and faith unfeign'd;

1 Chron. xxix. 20.
Ps. lxxvi. 12.

Gave the lilies and the leopard
　　Willing us, by that his shield,
Brave, our all for Christ to jeopard,
　　Pure, as flowers of the field:
Such sweet savour by his favour
　　May we to the Father yield.

Judges v. 18.

G

We the College of his founding
    Heirs of Eton's honour'd name,
Thee intreat, that sin abounding
    Bring her not with us to shame;
Bless Thou ever our endeavour,
    Prosper, Lord, her use and fame.

Through the night of our probation
    Earnestly to God we pray,
That we fail not of salvation
    Keeping well the narrow way:
Forward straining, ever gaining
    Glimpses of the eternal day.

So may grace divine prevent us
    Till be won our earthly fight,
And our King and Saint present us
    To his Sovran in the height,
For those gracious words of welcome
    Enter ye your Lord's delight.

Matt. xxv. 21.

Answering thus the call of duty,
    Rendering unto God our best,
May the King in all his beauty
    There to us be manifest;
In the very far off country
    May we all in Him be blest.

Is. xxxiii. 17.

Praise to God on high be given,
　To the sole begotten Son,
To the Spirit, as in heaven
　So on earth be homage done,
Glory, blessing, love addressing
　To the eternal Three in One.　AMEN.

CHISWICK PRESS : CHARLES WHITTINGHAM AND CO.
TOOKS COURT, CHANCERY LANE, LONDON.